18
SUMMER

THE Nightwatchman
THE WISDEN CRICKET QUARTERLY

Managing editor: Matt Thacker
Editors: Tanya Aldred, Anjali Doshi
Editorial board: Charlotte Atyeo, Matt Thacker, Tanya Aldred, Anjali Doshi, Jonathan Wilson, Lawrence Booth

Contact: editor@thenightwatchman.net or help@thenightwatchman.net
Website: www.thenightwatchman.net
Facebook: The Nightwatchman
Twitter: @NightwatchmanXI

Subscriptions: subscriptions@thenightwatchman.net

All advertising, sales, press and business communication should be addressed to:
contact@thenightwatchman.net or
The Nightwatchman, TriNorth Ltd, 4th Floor, Bedser Stand, The Kia Oval, Kennington, London SE11 5SS

Design and illustration: Joe Provis, TriNorth Ltd
Photography: Getty Images unless stated.
Typeset in Gotham

Printed and packaged by ACP for All Out Cricket Limited on behalf of John Wisden & Co Limited

The Nightwatchman is printed on paper certified by the Forest Stewardship Council

WISDEN, WISDEN INDIA and the device/logo of two cricketers in top hats are trademarks of John Wisden and Co Limited, a wholly owned subsidiary of Bloomsbury Publishing Plc

ISSN 9772052188005
A CIP catalogue record for *The Nightwatchman* is available from the British Library

THE Nightwatchman
THE WISDEN CRICKET QUARTERLY

Buy the 2017 Collection and receive a free
Cross Nile ballpoint pen worth £25

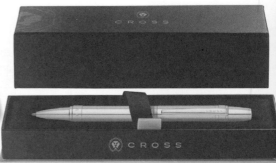

www.thenightwatchman.net

ISSUE 18 – SUMMER 2017

Purveyors of Great Sports Writing

Since 1864

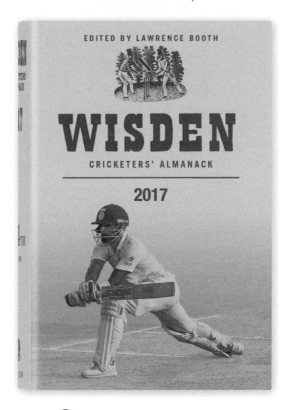

OPENERS

I'm looking out of my Kia Oval office window as preparations for the ICC Champions Trophy go on apace. The murmur of mowers, the banging of builders, the one-two, one-two sound checks, and the palpable and growing excitement all point to the fact that a big event is about to take place. And then, a much bigger event takes place. Young girls attending a concert in Manchester are targeted and killed in a terrorist attack.

We're almost inured to these atrocities. We pride ourselves on our stoicism; in our ability to keep calm and carry on; to dust off the gallows humour; to show solidarity with our hashtags, our balanced views and our Britishness. But this one is different. My cousin's girl was there, her friend's dad still in hospital, body shrapnel-pocked. A friend of a friend is still missing. And there's only one thing that means. And the greater-than-usual impotent rage this time around is not just because there's a personal link. It's because it's the slaughter of innocents, people who hadn't yet had a proper go at life. Utterly senseless, utterly stupid.

So we hang on to the wreckage, to the things we hold dear. The big things – friends, family, love, a life well-lived – and the fripperies, the meaningless things that mean so much, that distract us from reflecting on what this world is becoming. For those young kids it was Ariana Grande; for many of us it's cricket. Watching it, playing it, reading about it, imbuing it with significance.

This issue of *The Nightwatchman* has been finalised against this backdrop.

We hope we manage again to bring some joy into your lives, to entertain you for an hour or three, to make you reflect, to discover, to laugh and to rejoice that this thing we all love has the capacity to enthrall us still.

Within these pages, there is poetry, fiction, reminiscence, rumination, whimsy and lots of lovely pictures. We hope there is plenty in there to make you smile.

I'd also like to pay tribute here to Charlotte Atyeo, who leaves *The Nightwatchman* after this issue. It was Charlotte who came up with the name, who brought the team together, who generated so many ideas, who – with infinite patience – dragged us kicking and screaming to every deadline, who is common-sense personified, and whose editing is as good as it gets. If The Nightwatchman has its faults, they have not been of her making. I'm not sure what we'll do without her but, in keeping with the theme of this piece, we'll soldier on.

If you would like to write for us or just let us know what you think about *The Nightwatchman*, good or bad, please get in touch with us at editor@ thenightwatchman.net. We read every submission (but promise nothing) that fulfils our criteria: that articles should touch on cricket (however tangentially) and are original, well written and thought-provoking.

Matt Thacker, June 2017

Bert Oldfield films the England team walking onto the pitch

"TEAM ARRIVES IN NAPLES RAINY BUT HAPPY"

Imaginary travels with the 1930 Australian XI by Yvette Walker

25 April 1930

George. It's almost midnight on Anzac Day. We arrived at the Midland Grand Hotel, St Pancras, two days ago. As majestic as it is, it is not the legendary Hotel Cecil that the Australian players called home in previous years. The press are coping with no longer being in the West End, all except the *Herald's* Geoffrey Tebbutt, who seems to be taking the demolition of the Cecil as a personal insult. But as the majority of this Australian XI has never been to England, most would never have seen a hotel this opulent. The corridors stretch on for miles, all look the same and are so dimly lit that on our first evening here Fairfax and Bradman had to be rescued by bellboys and shown to their rooms.

On their first day in London there was a reception for the players at Australia House, and a luncheon with the British Sportsmen's Club at the Savoy Hotel. The Duke of Gloucester read a message from the King. In the afternoon the Australian XI had their first "shoulder-opening" practice at Lord's. There was a sea of press there, as well as British Pathé and Cinesound. Today there was an Anzac Day reception at Australian House, followed by a luncheon given by the Institute of Journalists. But I am getting ahead of myself. I will begin, where we all must, at the beginning.

On 24 March I met up with Jack Bridges from the *Daily Standard* at Perth Town Hall. We were there to report on the Lord Mayor's civic reception for the Australian XI. There was a new crop of teetotallers in the team, bringing the total number of abstainers to 12. Most of the players went straight for the

tea or the ginger beer, following the lead of their new captain Bill Woodfull, while the whisky and the Swan Lager were drunk by the journalists and the politicians; maybe Vic Richardson had one glass. These new players were young, that was for sure. Stan McCabe the youngest at 19, Archie Jackson 20, Don Bradman 21, Eddie a'Beckett 22. Jim Sadler from the *Mirror* mumbled "Woodfull's kindergarten," under his breath while he helped himself to a glass of hard liquor. His assessment of the newly appointed 1930 Ashes cricketers jarred with the slightly desperate slogan adapted by the team and trotted out at the reception by their manager, Bill Kelly: "In the bright lexicon of youth there is no such word as fail."

True, true – but there was also, in this team, no such word as experience, only four of the 15 players had played against an English side. And England had Wally Hammond, who'd destroyed the Australian bowling in 1928–29. The question on everyone's lips was: "Where is Jack Ryder?" Ryder had been on the selection committee, but that hadn't stopped the committee from handing the captaincy over to Woodfull. We couldn't understand it. Then there were the crates of ducks that had travelled, like a bad omen, on the same transcontinental train as the players. Woodfull and Richardson, waiting at Adelaide for their connection to Perth, tried to talk to the press while mobs of ducks gabbled behind them. We all wondered if the ducks were bound for the ship to England, but to the relief of both the press and the players alike, their tags revealed they were headed for somewhere called Northam in Western Australia.

Bridges, Sadler and I shared a car from Perth to Fremantle. The SS Orford would sail from Fremantle that evening with both players and pressmen on board. In the car we threw around what we knew about Woodfull's kindergarten. Archie Jackson had already given Larwood a pasting, but comparisons to Victor Trumper (we all agreed) were a bit premature. Bill Ponsford was as miserable as a bandicoot at the best of times, and right now was not the best of times for his batting. He would have to clear his head while at sea. McCabe held great promise with the bat and we desperately needed his medium pace. Apparently he was also a great dancer, so the young ladies of the *SS Orford* best beware. Eddie a'Beckett was an all-round talent on the field, a law student amongst sports goods salesmen, but it was doubtful he would gain a place in a Test side. Then there was Bradman. Bradman loved ice cream, the piano, and tennis. His 452 not out against Queensland was remarkable but we wondered how his unorthodox style would go under English conditions. We knew that the new players had bought a gramophone in Launceston and it had travelled all the way across Australia with them. Unlike the ducks, it would be with them on the ship bound for England.

On our second evening at sea, the Australian XI team manager Bill Kelly called a press conference in the F Deck Lounge. No players were present, only Kelly and Bill Ferguson, the team's scorer and baggage man. Kelly put several copies of the Australian Board of Control contract on the bar. We'd all read this astounding document. Convicts had more freedom, was our opinion of its 36 clauses. This comprehensive agreement between the players and the board governed eating, drinking, smoking, wives, children, mother-in-laws, unspecified visitors, unexpected death, fares, luggage, official engagements, punctuality, finance, blazers, caps and ties. Of course we were summoned to the bar so Kelly could draw our particular attention to Clause 11. This banned the Australian XI from speaking to journalists while en route to England. Here it is in full:

11. Neither the manager, treasurer, nor any player shall accept employment as a newspaper correspondent or do any work for, or in connection with any newspaper or any broadcasting, and no member of the team other than the manager shall directly or indirectly in any capacity whatsoever communicate with the Press, nor give any information concerning matters connected with the tour to the Press or any member, servant, or agent thereof.

Kelly, contract in hand, made it quite clear that we were forbidden to "have words with the players" until we reached St Pancras; then we could fire away. Therefore, when we disembarked at Naples to make our way across the Continent, all journalists were expressly forbidden to travel in the same rail compartment as the players. Kelly said (and I quote), "We will just be a party of ordinary Australians on a private trip, not wanting publicity. These players are young, with a great task ahead of them. I want to give them some privacy before the whole world comes down on their heads." Players and pressmen could be civil, Kelly continued, but no one would

be making any public statements until we reached the Midland Hotel. Kelly then bought us all a round of cheap drinks, the bastard.

With one little clause Kelly and the Board of Control had effectively confiscated our correspondent credentials for well over a month. As Bridges pointed out, we were being reduced to the status of female correspondents at a fashion show; we could observe the players, comment on their clothes and their hobbies and pastimes, but we couldn't actually speak to them. With our player contact effectively strangled, I prophesised we would spend the voyage fighting over scraps of news.

Later that same evening Bridges and I met in the Bamboo Bar to get well and truly drunk. I slipped my cigarette case onto the table. A waiter brought me an ashtray and I ordered four martinis. Bridges took a cigarette out of my case, lit the damn thing, and then he produced an Owzthat tin from his jacket pocket. He opened the little blue tin and took out the barrel dice (one for batting, one for bowling), also the Rules for Playing. A good game of schoolboy cricket would help us through this; there would be an epic struggle between my Australian XI and his International Musicians XI.

Count Basie won the toss and put Woodfull's men into bat and the marvellous and rather lovely Elsie Carlisle had some quick success, grabbing two wickets. A spirited fightback ensued but some excellent work in the second session by the slow medium Louis Armstrong kept the Australians in check. By this point, it was getting on to midnight. I was just about to order more drinks when Jim Sadler breezed past our table and mumbled, "Bradman is in the first-class lounge playing the piano."

We weren't so drunk that we couldn't make our way up to B Deck. Our press passes persuaded the first-class pursuer we weren't gawkers and he let us into the lounge. Bradman was indeed at the piano. Seeing that little bloke at that big piano made me appreciate for the first time just how small he was; small hands, small feet, twinkly eyes and a crooked smile. He was playing "Happy Feet" and the public were up and dancing. It was common knowledge that Bill Woodfull and some of the other Australia players did not dance at all; but I spotted Archie Jackson, Stan McCabe and Vic Richardson on the dance floor. Tim Wall, Alec Hurwood and Percy Hornibrook sat watching, sipping their ginger beer like country kids at a city dance. The ship's orchestra were looking very grateful for this unscheduled break, and were taking the opportunity to sit down and drink as much as they could before Bradman stopped his one-man show. Bradman was a fine player, quick and nimble but not too showy, quite polished. His little hands were flat and steady on the keys, his fingers drove the playing but it seemed to me that it was from his wrists that his talent kicked in – I can't quite describe it. I can only say that he took joy in what he was doing, and he did what he was doing very well. We stayed for quite a few numbers – Bradman was really enjoying himself. "Shout for Happiness" really got the dancers going, so once that was finished Bradman decided they needed a slower tempo and gave us his rendition of "Blue Skies". By

this time, Bridges was way past drunk and would have staggered up to Vic Richardson to ask him a question or two had Sadler and I not steered him through the lounge and out of there. And with that I had my first headline: "Bradman Plays Piano in Lounge."

A few days later Bridges, Sadler and I were up on the boat deck sitting under the morning sun. Bridges was asleep in his deckchair, Sadler was trying to fashion a news story out of not much at all, while I was reading Vicki Baum's *Grand Hotel*. I had brought ten novels with me and was looking forward to having the time to read them. I was drinking mineral water chased down with ginger beer (too many martinis the night before, like that time with you, George, on leave in Edinburgh). We were working, really. The Australian team had been horribly industrious all morning.

They'd been running around the boat deck in packs of two or three since six a.m., making a game of dodging young cricket fans who seemed to lie in wait for them every few feet or so. Ponsford worked particularly hard as he had to lose ten pounds before the series began. After the team exercise, and not content with an hour or so of brisk running on his own, Ponsford spent another hour throwing medicine balls at Richardson. Richardson egged him on by laughing at him. Later in the morning, McCabe (sporting a lovely light-blue bathing costume) did laps in the tiled pool. Fairfax joined McCabe, and so did Bradman, who couldn't swim but Fairfax had agreed to teach him.

By lunchtime the Australians had all left the boat deck. McCartney, Bardsley and Maley – ex-cricketers and now pressmen – turned up for a chat. They wanted to know what we were going to do about the press ban. Sadler ignored them and kept writing his story. Bridges opened his eyes at this point, not happy. I put my book down. What did they suggest we do? Ignore it? Rally our journalistic brethren? Get the Press Association to "strongly object"? They began to mutter at this point. Bridges, quite awake now, put his oar in – did they really want to be responsible for a player being fined, or worse, being left out of a Test because he broke the conditions of his contract? We could tell by the looks on their faces that no, they did not. "Gentlemen," I said, "it's a beautiful day. We are in the middle of the ocean on a very fine ship. You really should enjoy yourselves." And with that I went back to Vicki Baum. But Maley was persistent. What the bloody hell were they supposed to write about? Bridges closed his eyes again, a tired expression on his face. "Fairfax Teaches Bradman to Swim," he said. McCartney, Bardsley and Maley turned on their heels.

Then Sadler (still writing) mumbled something about Clarrie Grimmett being holed up in his cabin working on a book. I said he couldn't be. Sadler shrugged and said that was the rumour going around. And he wasn't writing poetry – he was working on an instructional manual on bowling technique. Well you know me, George. I bid Sadler and Bridges adieu, snapped shut my novel and went to investigate. There was a little bar on B Deck with a small lounge where some of the Australian players liked to sip their tea and their ginger beer or, if they were feeling adventurous, a sherry. Bert

Oldfield was there, writing a letter. With him were Ponsford, Alan Kippax and Richardson. Autograph hunters of both sexes milled around, their autograph books on full display, but they were hesitant to ask the players to oblige due to the order from the ship's captain banning such requests. I was glad there was a crowd, as this meant I could just slip into a nearby seat on the QT.

Eavesdropping (regardless of what you might think, George) doesn't come naturally to this journalist. I was no spy, no orphan in the British Raj, no Kimball O'Hara. I ordered a heart starter, opened my novel and pretended to read. Things started dully enough. Richardson teased Oldfield about the number of times he had written to his wife since he left New South Wales. Oldfield teased Richardson about the number of times he *hadn't* written to *his* wife. This made Vic laugh quite out loud. Oldfield had his film-camera on the table and Ponsford asked him if he'd shot anything that morning. "Bradman drowning," said Oldfield. The whole table laughed (except Ponsford). Oldfield said he hadn't shot much on the ship. Film was expensive; at only a couple of minutes a cartridge it was damn expensive. So he was saving film for Colombo, Cairo and the Continent. "Hey, that's a good title," Kippax said, "Someone write a jazz song. Bert, you've got paper and pen there. Off you go, mate. Could be a new career for you once you hang up the gloves."

Oldfield ignored Kipper's quip and asked Richardson if he thought Bradman would come good on English wickets. Richardson put his hands up and shook his head. "I wouldn't have a bloody clue. Has anyone had a good chat to Braddles since we left Perth?" No one had. It seemed that when Bradman wasn't playing the piano, or exercising with the team, or playing deck tennis, he was writing in his journal or was in his cabin listening to music. "He's not writing," Ponsford said. "That's what Mutt says anyway." According to Ponsford, Woodfull had tried to engage Bradman in some conversation by asking him about his journal and Bradman, deferring to his captain, showed him.

The page Woodfull was shown was full of figures: the number of miles from Perth to the Equator, the ship's speed, the length of the ship, the gross tonnage, the dead weight, the number of crew, the number of passengers. "Mutt loves his mathematics," Ponsford remarked, "but even he thought it was a little odd." Oldfield stopped writing his letter and chimed in. "Yes, that is odd, like Braddle's unorthodox batting, but look what he achieves. Perhaps it's part of why he can concentrate for such long periods of time." Richardson asked Oldfield what he meant and I'm glad he did because, as you know I'm not a bloody idiot, but I was losing the thread of the conversation. Oldfield explained: "Any of us going out to bat in a Test can't be looking at the lovely clouds, or the blades of freshly mown grass, we have to ignore what the barrackers have to say, we have to shut the whole world out. All that matters is the ball, and the fielders. We all have our own tricks, our own regime, some of us don't even know what we do exactly, we just do it. Perhaps Bradman does it by paring back the world to bare facts and figures. Maybe, to Bradman, the whole world is a ball-by-ball proposition."

There was some silence after this remark, which again I was grateful for, as I was trying to take in what Oldfield had suggested. Kippers was the first to throw his hat in, suggesting that what Oldfield meant was that a first-rate batsman could not also be a first-rate poet, he could only be one or the other. Oldfield nodded and the conversation turned to matters of the tour: hotels, tickets, baggage, laundry, train journeys. I snuck away quietly, none the wiser about Grimmett and his alleged writings, but there was food for thought in what I had heard.

I went down to C Deck. I wanted to spend some time in the writing room, to gather my thoughts and make some notes. As I strolled along an almost empty promenade deck, who should I come across but Bradman, sitting alone, drinking tea, his journal beside him, also copies of HV Morton's *In Search of England* and *The Nights of London*. Bradman said to me, "Beautiful day, isn't it?" I stopped at his feet, took off my hat, but I had no idea what to say to him, what I could say to him. I stood there like a dingbat. "Robert Atwood of the *Sporting Globe*," I said. "I'm just on my way to the writing room." Bradman said, "Stick around for a bit, Atwood. Kelly will be alright. I've had one or two words with some of the other press blokes on this trip. As long as we stick to trivial matters, no harm done." I nodded, but I still couldn't say a word. Don't take this the wrong way, but it was like trying to ask a girl out to the pictures, I couldn't string a sentence together. I'd talked to hundreds of sportsmen (and a few sportswomen) in my life, but the Board of Control ban had me jumpy and out of practice.

Bradman sipped his tea and didn't seem uncomfortable at all. He asked me to join him, so I sat down. I put my novel and notebook down on the deck, took off my hat. Bradman asked me my opinion on Morton's books and I said they were wonderful, a first-rate way to get to know England and the English way of life. He asked me if I was Australian Imperial Force. and I said yes, 29th Infantry Battalion, then the 32nd. I told him how water was so scarce in the trenches, we would use our hot tea ration to shave with – well, I did anyway. I said to Bradman that the Australian players were enslaved to their tea. Bradman chuckled and agreed. He said that their unofficial team slogan was "Win the Test with tea!" He didn't think the Australian team would last very long without tea. "Do you want to see how I take my tea Atwood? It's become a bit of a joke amongst the team." Bradman brought his tray around in front of him and got busy with the tea things. "No one can brew it the way I like it, you see. First, I fill my cup with a third of milk… Then I add a depth of half an inch or so of tea from the pot… Then I go on filling the rest of it with hot water. See?" He showed me the tea. It was the most anaemic brew I had ever seen. It looked like someone had dissolved chalk in hot water. "I wouldn't ask anyone else to make it like this for me. I take it as it comes in hotels, but the tea I really like is the one I brew myself. This is the oddest place I've ever made a cup; on the deck of an ocean liner, but I'm quite enjoying myself." Bradman did look happy, sitting on the deck with his insipid tea, the sunlight flicking over his young face. You and me, George, we were young like him once. I told Bradman I'd really enjoyed his performance in the lounge, particularly his playing of "Shout for Happiness". Bradman smiled. He started to hum the tune like he was Fred Astaire; then he winked at me and nudged me in the ribs as if to say, come on pal, sing! So, just for the hell of it, I sang "Shout for Happiness" with Don Bradman as we sailed towards the Equator on our way to England; on our way to a defeat, most likely, at the hands of the old enemy.

The ship continued on and so did the reporting from a discreet distance. Richardson, dressed as Neptune, was thrown into the pool just as we reached the Equator. Bradman beat Alec Hurwood in the deck-tennis final 6-1, 7-5. Tim Wall, Grimmett and a'Beckett bowled in a light-hearted way at some of the passengers in a game of deck cricket. Oldfield, when not writing to his wife, played bridge. Grimmett was a keen photographer. Hurwood was so shy that the team made it their mission to "bring him out." At the Gala Dance, some of the younger members of the team sported grease paint moustaches, painted on for a laugh by Grimmett.

At Colombo, a Ceylon XI did well to draw with the Australians – it was so hot the Australians batted in pith helmets. Once through the Suez Canal, which Oldfield saw fit to film, the Australians travelled from Port Said to Cairo to see the Sphinx and the Pyramids – there was a plague of locusts and grasshoppers while they were there, the natives banging kerosene drums to drive the insects away. The camels shook their bones up quite considerably and the team returned to the hotel happy but quite beaten up by the experience. I went out with the players to see the Pyramids, as the last time I was in Egypt I was too busy digging trenches with you – though, George, we rode the trams of Alexandria quite a bit, I recall. We left the ship for good at a rainy Naples, and the team arrived in Rome on Good Friday. Bradman bamboozled the Italian waiters by asking for tea at breakfast. The joke of the day amongst the team was that their thoughtful Methodist captain now had a thousand Catholic churches to recommend to his Catholic players. The Australians hustled through Rome, visiting the Forum, St Peter's, the Vatican, the Appian Way and the Catacombs.

On the train line between Milan and Lucerne we saw a rugby match being played under the Apennine mountains. Two thousand people gathered in the rain to watch. I don't know exactly where we were. It had been raining ever since we left the ship at Naples and things were becoming a little fractious in our railway compartment full of pressmen. It had been over three weeks and there was still very little real news to report – we kept cabling the same guff back to Australia. To make matters worse, since we landed our ranks had swelled somewhat, with journalists travelling from London to join the party, even though they had been warned not to come because of the ban on interviews. One silly sod spent the whole day traipsing around Pompeii with the Australians, thinking his dogged determination would get him some news; when all he got was soaking wet and a bit part in our news reports that evening. So, against all natural instincts, we decided to share our information and to spill everything we had on the Australians. I'm telling you, George, it was a little like our old Carlton gang at three in the morning, emptying their jacket pockets and coming up with half-broken cigarettes,

a couple of bob, an old slip from a Flemington bookie, and the grubby stub of a pencil. In other words, try as we might, we all came up with nothing of real value.

The only real news concerned Grimmett and his book on bowling. It seemed that in the three and a half weeks at sea he'd done more writing than the lot of us put together. By keeping himself to himself he'd managed to dash off a small instructional text entitled *Getting Wickets*. Tebbutt knew this, as it was Tebbutt who had typed up Grimmett's scribblings on his old jalopy of a typewriter. None of us had cottoned on to this cosy arrangement. Tebbutt finally spilled the beans and told us that both Kelly and the Board knew about the book. Before the tour began, Grimmett had sought written permission from the Board to enter into a contract to write his book and they had granted it. We all agreed we could add this story to our next cable. Then someone from Queensland dropped in a rumour that Bradman was considering writing a book. No one could confirm it though, so we decided to keep it under our hats. Sadler came up with the coup of the tour: he had it from Kelly that when the Australians arrived in Paris in a few days they would become the first cricket team to make a talkie. Oldfield had the film camera, and Kelly would shoot the sights and sounds at their Paris hotel. That really got the pressmen going and so our little chinwag began to break up. I could see the headline forming in the smoke filled air: "Australian XI To Break Silence in Paris".

Sadler left us for the dining car and his favourite bar stool, Bridges and I took our whisky bottle back to our seats and got stuck into what was now the world's longest Test match: day 16 of Australian XI v International Musicians XI. It was a monumental match – each side had batted and bowled five times. So far, the Australians had made a combined total of 546 runs while the Musicians were in the lead with 858. The match was tight, with no end in sight. Players on both sides were getting a little tired and there had been some injuries, but we urged our teams to play on as Bridges was bored and I was in need of distraction.

As our train swept through the rainy day, you flickered just outside my vision. You and me, George, we played schoolboy cricket too but we didn't have a fancy blue tin with barrel dice; all we had were two six-sided pencils and a tattered notebook. Atters' XI v George's XI, a roaming global Test match played on troop ships, in bars and when we were out of the line. I still have the notebook. We were still playing even after our troop ship got knocked about by a torpedo and we ended up clinging to the heel of Italy. We played on the troop train which took us to Nice, Monte Carlo, Marseille and then directly to Cherbourg (no Paris for us); we kept playing on the troop ship which took us to England and training on Salisbury Plain. Do you remember, George, on leave in Andover, rummaging in that musty old bookshop, the sherry-soaked bookseller told you not to smoke over the books after you'd dropped ash on her precious stack of *Boy's Own Papers*? I bought you a nice edition of *War of the Worlds* and you bought me a new book, *A Portrait of the Artist as a Young Man*. I hadn't read James Joyce before. When training ended, we were too late

for Gallipoli, so they shipped us off to the Somme. George, when something happened at the front and we couldn't figure out how to talk about, we'd just end the conversation by saying *Narpoo*; a corruption of "il n'y a plus" meaning "there is no more," or "nothing left." This could literally mean there are no more rations, or it could mean there is nothing left of me. George, I came home in 1918. I came home 12 years ago and things are still *Narpoo*.

When our Italian train reached Lucerne, Kelly and his off-sider Howard went by themselves to Interlaken, while a gang of pressmen, including Bridges and me, trailed after the players who were going to Vitznau. The Swiss pulled out a rather dodgy cogwheel railway engine so the players could travel up the mountain and have lunch at a hotel high up on the peak. None of us had seen anything like this before; the mountains crusted with snow, the magnificent lake below us, everything shining in bright sunlight. We climbed very, very high in an overloaded rattling engine. At one particularly tricky point I thought bloody hell, the Germans didn't kill me but the fucking Australian cricket team are going to. By the time we got to the top we were all as giddy as schoolgirls. Within minutes of us disembarking from the little train a snowball fight had started. It was infectious, all of us joined in, except Oldfield who was filming the whole spectacle. A natural split occurred in our ranks and soon the game was tribal – journalists v cricketers. A well-executed attack from the flank by the press had the players up against it for a while, but being who they were it didn't take them long to rally and soon we were on the defensive. When it all got a bit serious, Vic Richardson took it upon himself to take the heat out of our throwing arms. He stood on the brink of a 6,000-foot drop down into the lake and challenged anyone to hit him. We all had a go and I must say he dodged most of the snowballs with the agility of a boxer avoiding a right jab. Poor Wall nudged a German tourist during the horseplay, and the German's cigar popped out of his mouth and onto the snow. The man poured forth with the most colourful rant – we assumed he was swearing in a most spectacular way at Wall who was mortified at what he had done; but one of the press with passable German said that the man was demanding money in compensation. Wall obliged and an international incident was averted. As we all made our way to the hotel for lunch, Oldfield clapped Wall on the shoulder and said, "Careful, sunshine – that kind of thing is just how wars start." The sunny day, the snowballs, the absurdity of it all was a tonic for everyone. I think for all of us – players and press alike – it was the best day we had had since we left Perth three weeks before.

In Paris the Australians placed a wreath at the tomb of the Unknown Soldier. The wreath was bound with the Tricolour and the colours of the Australian cricket team. Bridges and Sadler and other press went with them. Later that same day the team went to the races at Saint-Cloud and won £300! They had a tip and they all bet on an Australian horse with an Australian jockey. Lucky bastards. The talkie that was supposed to be filmed at the hotel by Oldfield did not happen. Kelly said the players were too shy, but Bridges and I think Paris had challenged their teetotaller ways and they'd had quite a night of

it – perhaps not drinking, but plenty of carousing. Three hundred quid would have bought a lot of ginger beer.

After we disembarked at Dover and boarded the boat train, Kelly got us all to move into the players' carriage. He explained that due to the anticipated crowds at Victoria Station, the players' Pullman carriage would be detached from the boat train four miles out and hitched to a special engine. This is what they usually did for the royal family. Kelly said that barriers had been built to stop people coming onto the platform; and there were 100 policemen there in case the barricades didn't deter the more eager well-wishers. Kelly, Woodfull and the players would be met by Lord Plumer, President of MCC – yes, the very same General Plumer, "Old Plum" himself – as well as half a dozen English cricketers and representatives from Australia House. There would be a sizeable mob of photographers who would need to do their job, so the players would have to grin and bear it. Kelly would take several quick questions from the waiting press, then we would all make our way in an orderly fashion to the fleet of saloon cars which would take us to the Midland Grand Hotel.

As soon as we got off the train it was clear that the barricades and police had been a necessary idea – down the end of the platform were 4–5,000 people waiting to catch a glimpse of the 1930 Australian XI. The younger players were a bit taken aback by this, and were glad to make it safely to the waiting cars. We all piled into the vehicles with no particular order or method, the plan was just to get us to the hotel as quickly as possible. I shared a ride with Kelly, Woodfull,

Jackson and Kippax. I told Jackson that a young woman had somehow got onto the platform. She'd commented on how good-looking the players were. Jackson blushed and I said, "I bet you that will be in the papers tomorrow."

Today, at the Institute of Journalists lunch, Sadler, Bridges and I sat at a table with Vic Richardson and Bert Oldfield. Bridges couldn't help himself, telling Vic and Bert that now we were in London, he could finally ask the questions he'd been saving up for over a month, he only had 50 or 60, they wouldn't take very long to answer. On all the tables were ashtrays that read, "I am here for the Ashes." Woodfull gave a nice speech, in which he remembered the Anzacs. Sir Granville Ryrie, the Australian High Commissioner (in uniform as he had come straight from the Cenotaph) said that some thought this team to be too young, but he did not, as he could not forget what youngsters had done at Gallipoli. Then there was a silent toast for the Fallen. All of this remembrance, George, it is right and it is proper but I don't want anyone to become a statue, or a wreath, any more than the Australian XI would want to be reduced to statistics.

George, when we arrived in France I knew that I wanted to go back to the caves. So I left the cricketers and the pressmen and I took off out of Paris. I travelled the three hours by train to Naours. Once I was there I found someone who would guide me into the caves, someone with a good lamp who knew their way in and out of those tunnels and chambers. The going was slow. My guide cast his light on every inscription; there were hundreds of soldiers' names scrawled into the rock using bayonets, charcoal, pencils. I gave my guide no choice, I insisted he kept going – for hours, it seemed – and then all of a sudden we lucked on the one I was looking for:

29th Batt Australians July 1916

Robert Atwood and George Bennett

Carlton, VIC

Our names, George. Illuminated by the light, briefly, and then gone.

Author's note: This story could not have been written without Geoffrey Tebbutt's book With the 1930 Australians, *as well as numerous newspaper articles accessed via Trove, the online database of the National Library of Australia. I cheated with the recording date of the tune "Shout for Happiness" (written by Jack Hart & Tom Blight) by bringing it forward a year. The song was recorded in 1931 by Ray Noble and the New Mayfair Dance Orchestra (feat. vocals by Al Bowlly).*

• • •

SRI LANKA'S FIRST HEAD-HUNTER

Bharat Sundaresan recalls a meeting with a fast and furious pace bowler

On 27 February 1985, two West Indian batsmen retired hurt at the MCG. Both walked off spitting out blood after being struck on the mouth. Larry Gomes lost a few teeth; Richie Richardson had his jaw fractured and was sporting a golf-ball-sized lump on his right cheek by the time he was helped off the field. A few deliveries after Gomes was felled, Clive Lloyd nearly had his spectacles smashed before the back of his bat miraculously came to his rescue. The next over, the West Indian captain exchanged his sun hat for a helmet.

Now, this wasn't the first time that a West Indian batting line-up found themselves encountering remorseless hostility Down Under. They had come under fire a decade earlier when Dennis Lillee responded rather enthusiastically to the Australian crowd's calls of "kill, kill, kill". But here, on this muggy evening under lights in a rain-affected limited-overs international,

the indomitable West Indians were being held hostage by a couple of diminutive and affable Sri Lankans. David wasn't laying a few jabs at Goliath; he was knocking his teeth out – literally.

Ironically, one of the two bowlers dishing out the blows seemed at least as desperate as those receiving them. Rumesh Ratnayake was in tears after his full-length delivery shot up and smashed into Gomes' mouth.

However, his partner Ashantha de Mel – the first genuine pacer to emerge from Sri Lanka – wasn't prepared to give even a quarter. While he was concerned about Richardson's well-being, the fast bowler was reluctant to lose his "killer instinct". De Mel is surprised to learn that the video of him breaking the jaw of one of the Caribbean's most fearless batsmen still exists on YouTube – and has over half a million views. Not that he needs to watch a replay. Thirty years

on, images from that famous night in Melbourne are still very vivid. Seated comfortably in his aesthetically charming home, in the Wellawatte suburb of Colombo, the 58-year-old recalls the evening Rumesh and he "left world cricket in a state of shock".

"It was a lively pitch with dampness and the ball was skidding on. They underestimated us and tried to be a little too aggressive without realising," he recalls. "I didn't take any pride in breaking Richie's jaw. Someone can get seriously injured and you have to live with it for the rest of your life."

The Sri Lankans were comfortably beaten that evening by the mighty West Indians despite two "retired outs" on the scorecard. In the years to come, Sri Lanka would go on to become world champions and be counted among the top teams in the world. But that night, in the vast expanse of the MCG, the team experienced a seminal moment. A tiny island nation, branded "minnows", showed the world they could give just as good as they got.

During the 1980s, de Mel and co – a pace battery that also included Vinothen John and, later, Graeme Labrooy – would leave many more batting line-ups surprised by their speed and hunt-in-a-pack approach. But on that night in Melbourne, the Sri Lankan batsmen had suffered a fearsome battering by the West Indian attack, including Michael Holding, Malcolm Marshall, Joel Garner and Winston Davis – this after Duleep Mendis thought it wise to bat first despite the morning rain which had left the surface damp and fresh. By the time de Mel joined Ranjan Madugalle in

the middle, the top order had succumbed to the wicket's uneven bounce and Viv Richards's thrifty off spin. De Mel was quietly excited to be out there. He'd never faced Marshall and Holding.

Incidentally, his first impressions of Marshall didn't quite fit the reputation of the raging Bajan. "Marshall was bowling at me, and I was kind of playing him comfortably. I told Ranjan I don't know what the hype is about these guys. They're not that quick. Two balls later, one ball hit my helmet and then the sightscreen," he remembers with a chuckle. "I barely even moved."

It was the other end that de Mel was more interested in though. It's not often that an international cricketer experiences a fan-boy moment in the heat of battle. But as he stood at the non-striker's end, de Mel was so overawed by the sight of Holding running in to bowl that he stood with his back to the striking end, soaking in every second of "Whispering Death's" performance. Holding wasn't operating at full tilt either until one ball left Madugalle on his haunches.

"Michael bowled a ball that hit Ranjan full on his foot. He fell flat on the ground. It was that quick. Michael was walking past me and said: 'This was just to remind you that I can bowl quick once in a while,'" de Mel recalls, barely masking the admiration in his voice even three decades later.

Sri Lanka were already a Test nation by 1985. They'd been regulars at the 50-over World Cups too, but not many people took much notice of them. Neutral matches during the Benson & Hedges World Series Cup in 1985 – a tri-series involving Australia and West Indies – were often played on greentops where it was difficult to distinguish the pitch from the rest of the outfield. At a game in Hobart that season, the West Indians actually felt sorry for the Sri Lankans.

"I remember Garner on that wicket. The ball was flying off the surface. I used to feel for our opening batsmen," de Mel recalls, his expressive face breaking into a wry smile. "It was like they were going to war not knowing when or where they'd get shot or whether they would come back in one piece."

The MCG bloodbath convinced the West Indians they couldn't underestimate Sri Lanka, having received a taste of their own game. It also brought the likes of de Mel and Ratnayake into the spotlight and earned them plaudits from Holding and Garner.

De Mel had a languid action without a noticeable high jump before hitting his delivery stride. He was known more for his penchant to swing and seam the ball away from the right-hander. But he also had a deceptive enough bouncer that constantly put batsmen in harm's way. And hurt many of them too.

De Mel doesn't strike me as someone who once was a head-hunter with ball in hand. After his career ended prematurely at just 28 – owing to a terrible knee injury – he entered the apparel industry and ran his own garment factory. To keep his competitive juices flowing, or rather to cater to them, he turned to the more sedentary yet stimulating challenge of bridge. He got so good at it that it

took him to the Commonwealth Nations Bridge Championships in Manchester in 2002, making him probably only the second international cricketer after Everton Weekes to represent his nation at bridge. While the fast bowler-turned-bridge-player – as contrived as it sounds – still competes in World Championships, he spends most of his time trading in stocks and bonds. In fact, in present form, de Mel looks every bit the seasoned stockbroker rather than a cricketer who once broke Javed Miandad's hand and clocked Sandeep Patil on the head. There is no brazen glee in his tone when he talks about his various victims, but there is a sense of fulfilment for sure

"The first time I hit a guy in the head was in our first-ever Test against England at the P Sara Oval. Chris Tavaré opened. I bounced him and broke his helmet. Then in 1982 in India, I hit Sandeep Patil. He talks about it all the time. It was in a match at Chepauk. He got a hundred too. Once I met him with his son, and he told his boy: 'This guy hit me on the head.'

"Then on a tour to Pakistan in 1985, where they had Imran [Khan] and Wasim [Akram], I fractured Javed Miandad's hand. They were surprised that Rumesh and I were consistently bowling quicker than their fast bowlers, which was quite a feat."

By the mid-1980s, trouble had begun in the north and other parts of Sri Lanka. The Civil War had broken out. But it was also a time that club cricket was thriving in Colombo. That the four major grounds – the Sinhalese Sports Club,

Nondescripts Cricket Club, Bloomfield and Colombo Cricket Club – were all roughly within a one-kilometre radius, meant that cricket felt like Wimbledon in June with crowds constantly moving from one venue to another depending on who was batting or bowling at the time. While Sri Lanka possessed an array of easy-on-the-eye batsmen led by Roy Dias, it was the fierce rivalry between the four big fast bowlers – Messrs de Mel, Labrooy, Ratnayake and John – that caught the fancy of most locals. With each of the ball-toting baddies representing different clubs, there was never any shortage of action.

Here too, de Mel wasn't letting batsmen be at peace. Fans at the SSC would flock the hill – now replaced by administrative buildings – to see their hero bounce out the opposition on the paciest wicket in town. But there was stunned silence one afternoon when de Mel bounced Ajith de Silva, a left-arm spinner, and struck him on the head. De Silva enjoyed cult status regardless of club affinity and the crowd booed and pelted stones at de Mel. That wasn't the only physical danger he survived that day. "Ajith fell to the ground when the ball struck him," remembers de Mel. "But he immediately got up and started running towards me with bat in hand. It took a few players to jump on him and stop him in his tracks." The incident caused a mini-riot and required police intervention to restore order.

That Sri Lanka would prepare grassy tracks to welcome an opposition team, even India, seems unimaginable in the post-Muralitharan era. But that's what greeted the Indians on their 1985 tour. It was a three-Test series that led to Sri Lanka's first Test win – in the second game at the P Sara Oval – when de Mel took five wickets and played second fiddle to Ratnayake who finished with nine. The Sri Lankan pace trio of Ratnayake, de Mel and Saliya Ahangama captured 50 of the 52 Indian wickets in the series – the other two going to the canny medium-pace of Arjuna Ranatunga.

"The Indians didn't know what hit them. They were a full-strength outfit with everyone from Gavaskar to Vengsarkar to Kapil Dev. Mohammad Azharuddin landed here, having scored three consecutive centuries in England, and was a total flop. We ensured he didn't make even a 50.

"Back then, fast bowlers took wickets for Sri Lanka. People might not quite believe it thanks to the exploits of Murali and Rangana [Herath]. Now the focus is skewed in favour of spinners and spinning wickets," points out de Mel, who finished his 17-year Test career with 59 wickets at 36.94.

He took five wickets in the first Test at the SSC – his home ground – including Dilip Vengsarkar, Ravi Shastri and Kapil Dev. The disappointment of having to settle for a draw in the rain-affected first Test of the series was soon forgotten once the Lankans crossed the line a week later at the P Sara Oval. That it came against "big brother" India also meant a lot. But so confident were they of beating India that de Mel insists the arrack didn't quite flow as unabashedly as you would have expected. "After that Test win we could say: 'Yes, finally we have arrived and are on the stage with the world's best.'" The third Test in Kandy was drawn, which meant Sri Lanka had ticked off their first series win in Tests.

Seven months after having shown the world they wouldn't back down from anyone at the MCG, the Sri Lankan pacers had ensured that their nation could stand their ground against the world's best even in a format that they had been inducted into only three years earlier. De Mel was still in his early twenties when Sri Lanka toured England in 1981 and were accorded Test status soon after. Only a few years earlier, he had been named the country's best schoolboy bowler. He had also done well against an Australian under-19 outfit that included David Boon and Greg Dyer, but he thrived most on the seam and swing on offer in England.

When England landed in Colombo a year later to welcome the newest Test nation into the fold, de Mel had to see off competition from John and Ratnayake to get the nod as the solitary fast bowler – the country was yet to embrace its pacers. It meant he would be the first to bowl in a Test match for Sri Lanka. His impact was instant as he reduced England to 40 for 3 in the space of seven deliveries. His three wickets were Geoff Cook, caught at gully; Tavaré, hit on the head and bowled; and Graham Gooch, out leg before. He later added Ian Botham to his tally. If it were not for a catastrophic 8-for-7 collapse in the second innings, Sri Lanka would have made a better first impression than most other Test debutants. De Mel, meanwhile, had made an entry into the record books that will remain his forever.

He is no cricket tragic though. When you walk around his sizeable living-room it's difficult to see any conspicuous remnants of his cricketing past. But ask him about being the "first-ever" and he flashes a beaming smile even if he believes it was nothing more than "right place, right time".

"They could have opened with a spinner. If you go through Test history to see who bowled the first ball and took the first wicket for Sri Lanka, it'll always be me. Other records, number of runs and wickets can change."

Not long after, in October 1982, came the rebel tour to South Africa – one that inadvertently set off the pace revolution in Sri Lanka. De Mel was on the organisers' wish list but he declined the offer, saying he was too young to jeopardise his international career. It was a bold move when you consider that the Lankans earned one tenth of the money made by the West Indians – then the poorest-paid cricketers in the world. The pittance pay helped him make up his mind a few years later when a serious knee injury threatened to end his career in his late twenties. De Mel was a successful computer analyst by then: he would be on the road meeting clients and selling everything from the NBS 2200 to the IBM 34 (which would fill up entire rooms) while being harangued for autographs.

Such was the severity of the prognosis that de Mel needed surgery immediately, but it coincided with one of the worst periods in war-time Sri Lanka – an armed uprising by the Janatha Vimukthi Peramuna, or People's Liberation Front, that lasted from 1987–89. "My knee-cap was rubbing against my bone. They said I'd have to wait for a year and a half for a proper surgery because of the situation at home. They didn't have the facility or know-how for arthroscopic surgery. They would have to lift the knee-cap up and pin it so that there was no friction," he says. "If I wanted to play cricket again I needed the surgery. But it was also a lot of money and I could just live my life without it. It wasn't like now when the [cricket] board pays."

De Mel was 28 when he last played for Sri Lanka, but he hasn't spent the rest of his life moping about what could have been. He did enough in Sri Lanka's nascent years to ensure his team progressed more rapidly than most others in Test history.

Yet he wasn't done with cricket, and he took on two increasingly controversial stints as the chairman of the national selection panel. As with ball in hand, he developed a reputation for being a head-hunter, at least among the senior players, who lived in fear that he would come for them wielding an axe. Former Sri Lankan captain Marvan Atapattu and the outspoken de Mel had many sparring matches during the 2000s. Then, de Mel recalls, Sanath Jayasuriya wanted to keep playing into his forties despite struggling to get bat on ball: "When I dropped him, he became a minister and forced his way back into the team for

the ODIs. That's when I thought I had had enough with these guys."

De Mel still watches cricket in his off-time, though he's not obsessed with it, and takes pride in the fact that many of the players he picked during his reign as selector are now at the forefront of the country's cricketing future. But he claims to have no intention of ever being associated with cricket again. He's content with focusing on the stock market and playing the odd bridge tournament.

Not many sportspersons, especially those who retire young, get a second shot at representing their country on the world stage. And de Mel is incredibly proud to have walked under the Sri Lankan flag in Manchester during the Commonwealth Games.

"It's an amazing feeling to have your country's name next to yours on a global stage. But there's no comparison to standing at the top of your mark with a new ball in hand and then running in with the crowd screaming their lungs out."

Just as we're about to part ways, he has a request: "Can you share that YouTube link of my ball to Richie? I remember it vividly, but I don't mind seeing it again," he says, with that delightful Sri Lankan twang and the kind of glee you can only expect from a fast bowler – one who is yet to lose his killer instinct.

• • •

CLOSE ENCOUNTERS

Benj Moorehead was there when England's former captain went big in the States

I was a fledgling staff writer at the *Wisden Cricketer* magazine when my editor pulled me aside one morning. "So here's the deal: there's a West Indian expat community in Connecticut, USA, who want to induct Brian Close into their hall of fame. We've struck up a deal with Yorkshire to fly Brian and his wife to Boston, along with a member of our editorial team... assuming you want to go."

A fortnight later I was fidgeting nervously in an airport lounge, waiting for Mr and Mrs Close. I was encumbered by a plastic boot on my left foot because I'd injured myself playing football a few days earlier. It was an embarrassing situation. Brian Close was one of the toughest sportsmen who ever lived, a man who charged down the wicket to the great fast bowlers of the West Indies and thought pain was no more of an irritant than a fly: "How can the ball hurt you? It's only on you for a second." And there I was, a southern softie hobbling like a robot because of an innocuous incident in a friendly game of football. At least I could use it as an ice-breaker.

But, as I came to learn, there was never any ice to break with Brian; you were always straight in. In a flash the Closes had swept me up as if I was their grandchild, and on the escalators Brian's tongue was wagging about the 1964 tour to the USA, when Garry Sobers played for Yorkshire for the one and only time.

So began an unforgettable three days in America with Brian Close. For one Louis Theroux-style weekend, I lived in his pocket. In an enormous, sad shopping mall we worked our way messily through a stack of pancakes drowned in maple syrup. We drank midday whisky out the back of a jeep by a cricket field. We puffed behind restaurants (chain-smoking was part of the brief). He talked a lot of cricket.

People sometimes assume that the highlight of working in cricket is the big-name interview. Have you done KP? Tendulkar? Root? Botham? Richards? After all, big-name interviews sell (or at least are thought to). They are splashed across the cover of monthly magazines and the back pages of newspapers.

Interviewing sportsmen is a difficult and ever more demanding skill, and there are some talented practitioners who provide insightful portraits. But the breakdown in trust between the media and the players, the uber-professionalisation of cricket, and the monopoly of commerce have all meant that the modern interview is typically saddled with terms and conditions. Like patients at a clinic, journalists queue up for their ten-minute, one-to-one slot in an empty, soulless room at the back of a building. Sponsors will be lurking. Many of the players are "media trained" (the art of talking without saying anything) and will have been prepped to promote whatever "initiative" is on the agenda.

To think of a 24-year-old John Woodcock sailing across the Pacific on the Stratheden with the England team – including a 19-year-old Brian Close – for the 1950–51 Ashes. Or Frank Keating melting into the players' fraternity during the emotional tour of the Caribbean 30 years later. Embedded into a timeless, informal bubble, Woodcock and Keating really came to know the men they were writing about. And it was one hell of a ride too.

Going to America with Brian Close felt like a window into a more carefree age when there were few strings attached. True, I was not rubbing shoulders with England's premier cricketers like Woodcock and Keating had. My subject leaned on a walking stick and was prone to nodding off during speeches. But he was Brian Close, and he was all mine.

Yet, Brian was only part of the story. Hartford, the capital of Connecticut with around 125,000 residents, is ostensibly an unremarkable city of skyscrapers

and insurers. But a small infestation of cricket has broken out among the expat Caribbean community who make up around a fifth of the population. The first wave of immigrants came here to farm the tobacco fields in the 1940s, and what began as games of "catchy shooby" has flourished into a full-blown cricket association with half a dozen teams who play in the Connecticut Cricket League.

The story of immigrants using cricket to assert their identity in a foreign land is always seductive, but hardly unique. What makes Hartford different is its Cricket Hall of Fame, the first in existence when it was founded in 1981. It is run by a pool of middle-aged men from all over the Caribbean: Jamaicans, Barbadians, Trinidadians, Antiguans, Guyanese, St Kittians and Nevisians. "We played and created our own history," one member told me. "But what would happen after? We'd be forgotten. So we said: 'Let us have a hall of fame.'"

Each year the committee nominates two of the game's greatest names – with an unabashed bias towards West Indians – and invites them to its annual induction ceremony in Hartford. Amazingly, they come. Headley, the three Ws, Valentine, Gibbs, Hall, Sobers, Kallicharran, Lloyd, Garner, Roberts, Holding, Greenidge, Haynes, Richards. So too Gavaskar, Chandrasekhar, Engineer, Viswanath, Greig, Mushtaq Mohammad. (Even Usain Bolt made a cameo appearance featuring a 28-second speech, long by his standards.)

They are not invited for formalities. That is the whole point of getting these great players out to Hartford; so that they mix spontaneously with the locals, peer into

Hartford's cricketing history, and talk about their lives like they would among friends. "All these great players get the chance to come to Hartford and actually be with us," said Mike Chambers, a middle-aged Jamaican who has been the Hall of Fame's head honcho for the last 20 years. "We get to share some of their personal stories."

On Saturday morning Brian Close was taken to the Dunns River Restaurant on Main Street, downtown Hartford. No one would know it, but a shrine to cricket is tucked up on the second floor: the Hall of Fame itself. When Michael Holding walked in here he pointed to a spot on the floor. "I'll sit there," he said. It was a display of humility: "I am in your house. We are all one and the same here."

There was an extraordinary range of boots, bats, books and other curios, from the first trophy played for in New England in 1900 to Alf Valentine's cable-knit sweater donated by the player himself. A VHS of West Indies against Pakistan in 1993 was showing on a small TV set. Brian marvelled at the memorabilia which filled the walls. "There's nothing like this in any other part of the world," he said, pointing his walking stick at items of interest. It was such an assault upon the senses that you needed to pop out for some air – or a fag.

Then a hush came over the room as Brian pulled up a chair like a man waiting for his grandson to hop on his lap. For an hour he reached into his bottomless vault of cricketing memories, turning his walking stick into a bat whenever necessary. Tony Greig took a bit of a pounding ("Christ almighty, he didn't know what day it was!"), as did Colin Cowdrey ("When he replaced me as captain for

the 1967–68 West Indies tour, Colin kept ringing me up and asking what to do!"). There were a few in-my-day jibes ("If I ran the game I'd give the captains some right stick for faffing about with the ball instead of getting it back to the bloody bowler!"). We heard his version of the 1956 Idris Baig affair, in which he and other England players nearly caused an international dispute after kidnapping a Pakistan umpire (Mr Baig) in Peshawar and pouring buckets of water over him ("He was enjoying it. We told him it was what we did to all great umpires. If the Pakistan players hadn't turned up, everything would have been fine; we'd have been the best of pals.").

None of these asides were barbed, because nearly everything Brian said was immediately disarmed by that chesty cackle which invariably punctuated his stories. It had all been a bit of fun. For all the hardships he suffered in an extraordinary roller-coaster career, Brian appeared to begrudge no one and regret nothing, and would laugh off the setbacks. "I had one hell of a life," he would say. "I played some great matches against some of the best players in the world."

This was the kind of intimate two-way exchange the Cricket Hall of Fame revels in, what Chambers meant when he talked about the players "being with us". Brian had been imbibed with Hartford's cricketing history, and then he had poured forth the tales of his tumultuous career.

We took off to the evening's induction ceremony at the Marriot Hotel in high spirits. A curious range of figures sprung up all around us: a journalist and photographer from the *New York Times*; a Canadian who came for the posthumous induction of his great uncle, Frederick James Heather; former Indian captain Ajit Wadekar, the other headline inductee, a somewhat milder presence than Brian; Joseph O'Neill, author of the acclaimed *Netherland* and the man who had set off this chain of events by alerting Yorkshire to Close's nomination.

It was a strange, drawn-out glitzy affair. Close and Wadekar were not the only inductees. Around a dozen figures who had contributed significantly to American and Canadian cricket were also to be honoured. They were all sitting in a line on a raised platform facing the rest of us. For much of the evening Mrs Close and I worried about whether Brian was about to drop off and if he had anything planned for his speech. We needn't have fretted. When Brian's turn came he flickered into life and nonchalantly carried on where he'd left off at the Hall of Fame: "I won six Tests and drew one as England captain, so they sacked me." Cackle, cackle, cackle. And the house came down.

The best was still to come. On a beautiful Sunday, we were driven to Keney Park to watch an exotic brand of helter-skelter cricket played on a clay wicket surrounded by an overgrown outfield. A small local crowd were arranged haphazardly along the boundary and between the parked cars. Reggae boomed out from one corner, a vat of goat soup steamed in another, and plastic cups were being refilled with amber liquid. Jamaica in Hartford.

Brian turned up at Keney Park dressed for a walk over the dales with his terriers. He was mobbed. A small Trinidadian called Vernon launched into impressions of him coming down the wicket to put

off the West Indies fast bowlers Hall and Griffith at Lord's in 1963, a display of courage (or madness) which produced that famous picture of Brian's bruised torso. "How did you do that, man?" asked Vernon, eyes bulging, brow furrowed. "Oh that. That were fun," cackled Brian. Vernon's eyes bulged some more, and then he keeled over in stitches.

This was why Brian Close was here. His nomination might otherwise seem odd; he had played only 22 Tests, and was not the most prominent former England player alive. But West Indians have never forgotten his fortitude against their great fast bowlers, first against the pioneers Hall and Griffith, and then when he defied Holding, Roberts and Daniel at Old Trafford more than a decade later at the age of 45.

While the clamour continued around him, I looked at Close again. It had been too easy to become lost in the wrinkles of a 79-year-old man, in all the cackles and caricatures. For the first time I imagined the cricketer he once was. The 18-year-old who became England's youngest Test debutant in 1949. The young, awkward outsider on the 1950–51 Ashes tour, after which he was axed. The truculent captain of the Yorkshire team which dominated the 1960s. The unflinching fielder at very silly short leg. The anti-establishment man. The England captain sacked after being deemed guilty of time-wasting tactics in a County Championship match. Somerset's inspirational leader in the 1970s who nurtured the raw competitive juices of Viv Richards and Ian Botham. The middle-aged man who was called up by England for the tenth and final time in 1976 and withstood a bodyline assault from possibly the meanest pace attack in Test history with little to protect him save his wits. He played his last first-class game ten years later, aged 55.

He'd been through all of that, and now here we were, a few decades on, in Hartford, USA. It made me feel dizzy. I looked at Brian in awe just like everyone else at Keney Park.

The opening skirmishes concluded, we settled into a never-ending flow of cricket anecdotes accompanied by rum on tap. Brian had plenty more in the tank, and the Hartford spectators were more than a match. I tried to catch some of it on a dictaphone, but much of the sound is drowned out by a thumping reggae baseline.

It went on like this for several hours. Brian was in his element, talking to anyone who would listen. For all his entrenched Yorkshireness, he was amazingly adaptable, even in old age, breezing through an alien environment and making himself instantly popular. He got on with everyone. No one felt judged. I thought I caught a glimpse of what made him such a hit with a young Botham and Richards at Somerset. (Though it must be said that Brian also rubbed up one or two the wrong way in his 37 years as a cricketer.)

He tolerated me, a young north London softie with long hair who stumbled about in a plastic boot and kept popping up at every turn. I'm not sure he ever really knew my name – I was always "lad". But he accepted me and talked freely. That was enough.

But perhaps the real heroine of the tale was Vivien, Brian's wife of 49 years. She had lived through all the highs, lows and controversies of Brian's career. It surely required a stoicism of a different sort, but no less demanding. In Hartford she charmed our hosts with her grace and diplomacy while steering her husband through the onrush of events. She would spy Brian heading for a refill and seamlessly remove the empty plastic cup from his hand ("I'll do it, love"). She would withdraw him from the fold when it seemed Brian might talk himself to exhaustion.

Arriving back at Heathrow on Monday morning was like returning from Narnia through the wardrobe. There was a crushing anti-climax to the silence at home. It reminded me of how I felt after returning to my bedroom as a 12-year-old following a dalliance with Louise Tomlinson on a school ski trip: "Nothing will ever be as good as that ever again." I was wrong about Louise Tomlinson.

In the years since, former West Indian cricketers have continued to descend upon Hartford. Jeffrey Dujon, John Shepherd (with his 94-year-old mother), Courtney Walsh, Lawrence Rowe, Mansoor Akhtar, Stephanie Power, Basil Butcher, Joe Solomon and Deryck Murray have all come this way over the last six years. Colin Croft became the 100th inductee in 2014.

And the Cricket Hall of Fame is more than an indulgence of great Caribbean cricketers. Increasingly it has become a forum for debate on the state of cricket in the West Indies (a convoluted subject for another time) and in the US (even more convoluted). Last year's ceremony was attended by the president of West Indies Cricket Board, David Cameron. It beggars belief that all this has been achieved by a few enthusiastic expatriates on a shoestring budget.

Brian Close died in 2015, aged 84. Vivien had told me he would always eat fish and chips on Friday, and amid life's ups and downs I had found this to be a solid, reassuring thought come the end of the working week. It was discomforting to think Brian's fish-chip-Fridays were done. The consolation was that, as far I could tell, he died a happy man.

With thanks to Patrick Hamilton, Curtis Clarke, Stan Walker and everyone else at the Cricket Hall of Fame who showed us such a good time. And to Howard Ferguson of Yorkshire CCC who was minder to Brian while we were in Hartford.

• • •

SHABASH, SHABASH

Noah Levick on being an American obsessed with Pakistan cricket

Once upon a time in Barcelona, people treated me like God – at least the Pakistani immigrants did. They kissed my shirt, offered me cake, and begged me to take cans of Bud Light as I tried not to stare at topless women on the beach.

The reason for this adulation was my attire. I wore a bright green jersey with "Pakistan" across my chest, and a sweat-soaked hat with a yellow star. It wasn't a conscious decision, but I had started to kiss the star every time I took the hat off or put it on. I've never been much of a kisser, so this significantly increased my kiss-per-day average.

Some people just smiled at me, thanked me for taking their free stuff, and left. Others talked with me about Yasir Shah's emergence, about Pakistan's comeback in the first Test against Sri Lanka at Galle (this was 2015), about who should play in their upcoming series against England. Twenty-seven months later, I'm yet to make full sense of these interactions. And I am still unable to understand this bizarre, delightful phenomenon of becoming a deity for several days.

If I were Pakistani, my jersey and hat wouldn't have been noteworthy, let alone worthy of worship. But as a white kid visiting the first country of 12 on a three-week trip across Europe with my two friends, my unusual clothing elevated my status. The one thing the experience confirmed was that I should never stop being an obsessive fan of Pakistani cricket. While my friend snored below me on our Airbnb-supplied bunk bed, I racked up hundreds of dollars of data, watching cricket highlights on my phone.

• • •

I first watched Pakistan on 14 February 2015 – their opening World Cup game, against India, witnessed by a billion people. Pakistan lost, as they always do when playing India in the World Cup. I'd learned this information from Imad, a Pakistani friend who now marvels at how quickly my cricket knowledge has surpassed his own. I developed an addiction to the sport, watching every game Pakistan played in the tournament. I memorised field settings until they became second nature, and

absorbed strategies like farming the strike and making the most of the allotted two bouncers per over. I learned that Pakistani cricket is notoriously unpredictable, but I failed to absorb the impact that would have on me every day for the next two years.

After Pakistan's loss to Australia in the quarter-finals, Misbah-ul-Haq resigned from the limited-overs captaincy. While such a moment might typically produce watery eyes and a quavering voice, Misbah's announcement was unsentimental. When I saw the headline in my daily perusal of cricket news and watched the video of his speech, I felt an odd connection.

Misbah and I do not wear our hearts on our sleeves. His most positive emotion – reserved for special occasions – is a shy smile. His most negative emotion is a rub of the forehead, as though feeling for wrinkles that logic dictates should be abundant. We both sport substantial beards: his with distinguished speckles of grey, mine with speckles of red that will eventually become grey. We also speak in a monotone that, while often insufferable, hints at wisdom. We like to ponder permutations. We can't help but look stoic.

Misbah recently retired as Test captain. Given that he is 42 and presided in January over a shambolic 3-0 whitewash in Australia, rumours inevitably swirled about his future. It was no surprise to hear the West Indies series would be his last. I've savoured every run he's scored in his final few innings, especially the two consecutive sixes he blasted to score the winning runs for Pakistan in the first Test. I watched as Misbah characteristically ground down the West Indies bowlers, scoring 99 not out that could have been a special century if not for the inevitable failure of Mohammad Abbas, Pakistan's No.11.

Based on the intense scrutiny I have heard commentators heap upon captains during my all-night experiences watching Pakistan instead of sleeping, studying, or pretending I'm an extrovert, I have gained an appreciation for how difficult it is to lead a cricket team. I haven't always agreed with Misbah, but it's not easy to decide whether Sohail Khan deserves a fourth slip, if Rahat Ali should open the bowling in England or be first change or, indeed, when it's appropriate to put in a short leg for Yasir Shah.

To his credit, Misbah took Pakistan to the No.1 Test ranking last year – his ultimate triumph despite several obstacles, including the absence of cricket in his home country, the spot-fixing scandal of 2010, a meddling mother-in-law of a national cricket board, and his own flawed players (Wahab Riaz, for instance, who will win you a match one day and make you feel embarrassed for him the next).

As a batsman, Misbah is an acquired taste. Against fast bowling, he defends, smothering ball after ball with an ungainly half-stride and a disdain for all things aesthetically pleasurable. Against spin, he defends too, sometimes. In my early days as a fan, his style perplexed me – he seemed to be waging a war of attrition without the opposition's consent. I discovered that when Misbah makes up his mind, sometimes after two or three hours at the crease, he attacks the spin bowlers in a burst of acceleration. First, though, he waits, lets the ball travel into his arc, calculates the target's trajectory;

finally, he swings, as he hears the echo of ball on bat and stares at the battered piece of leather crashing into an empty seat in a mostly empty stadium in the desert of Dubai. A fan or member of the ground staff returns the ball, and he knows he must focus again on survival. Like Misbah, I live mostly in my own world, an American fan of Pakistan cricket who may never meet anyone who completely shares his obsession.

The polar opposite of Misbah is the one and only Shahid "Boom Boom" Afridi. He is like that cool kid in the neighborhood who spends all day at the skating rink, attracting a huge swarm of teenage girls who beg for his phone number, and an audience of wide-eyed little boys who worship his every move. Legend has it he landed a sick trick last July. Or maybe it was May? You must watch him, even if all he does is fall. Because when he stays on his feet, he's bold, graceful and transcendent. I cannot relate to this awesome coolness, but it's a treat to experience vicariously, even thousands of miles away, through a computer screen.

At the age of 16 (allegedly), in 1996, Afridi set the record for the fastest ODI hundred, in 37 balls. I tell my American friends this is like a high-school senior playing for an NBA team and scoring 65 points in his very first game. The grainy footage (on YouTube) from Pakistani television enhances the legend. On 19 February 2017, Afridi retired for the fifth and possibly final time.

I think part of my infatuation with Afridi stems from my own brief experience as a star. I always saw myself as the Tim Duncan of seventh- and eighth-grade basketball, never flashy but fundamentally sound and tenacious enough to use the temporary height advantage of early puberty to post 15 points and 20 rebounds. It was a weird feeling to know that, in a year or two, as the kids around me hit their growth spurts, I'd be forced to transition into a scrappy point guard for the rest of my life. But, for a couple years, my above-average stature allowed me to know the feeling of domination, to understand the pressure of swarming double teams and the power to single-handedly seize control of the game.

Now I often wonder what my life would be like if I hadn't stopped growing, if my array of post moves and uncanny rebounding instincts hadn't abruptly been rendered worthless. I like to think I would have continued to make the most of my height, that I would have been mature enough to avoid the frequent boneheaded failures of Afridi. Still, I imagine I wouldn't always have been able to resist the temptation to shoot just about every time I touched the ball, to attempt ludicrous behind-the-back crossovers and fadeaway three-pointers in the hope that, on a perfect day, I would score 85 points and give the crowd something they'd never forget.

It just so happens that my favourite player is only 5ft 8 (no, it's not Afridi or Misbah). Ever since I saw him restlessly shifting around the crease, imitating the Energizer Bunny in Pakistan's tense World Cup encounter against South Africa, I've loved Sarfraz Ahmed. I feel a kinship with him that is difficult to define; unlike with Misbah, we do not have much in common (besides our height, or lack thereof). Sarfraz is a "fighter", a "go-getter," a "hustler". In this way, he is a cliché: the stocky, feisty guy who makes the most of what he's got.

At a stout 5ft 5, I probably looked pretty similar to Sarfraz playing basketball, at least once I stopped growing around the age of 14. I got used to being the shortest guy on court, and revelled in every opportunity to play the role of the desperately diving, relentless player who manages to hold his own thanks to skill, heart, and hustle. I knew I was embodying a cliché, and I loved it. Outside sport, though, I would never want to morph into a cliché. My big beard (I haven't shaved in over four years), red sports goggles, and year-round shorts occasionally draw puzzled looks. I hate the idea of having to dominate the college beer-pong circuit every weekend and pump iron six days a week almost as much as I can't stand the thought of having to be a diligent student who actually enjoys 17th-century English literature or a nature worshipper who has to scale mountains and chomp on trail mix. But I'll be Sarfraz any day of the week.

Sarfraz is Pakistan's wicket-keeper – when I'm explaining cricket to novices I say that the wicket-keeper is like a catcher in baseball, even though this doesn't come close to capturing the intricacies of the position. He has also recently taken over the ODI and T20 captaincy. On some days, he crouches behind the stumps for 300, 400, 500 balls. He's not a quiet presence. His mouth is always moving: "Shabash, shabash, very well bowled yaar, just like that, shabash!" There are subtle, brilliant variations to this soothing refrain, I am sure, but this is essentially the Sarfraz soundtrack. Bravo, he is saying. Keep doing what you're doing. Be patient and trust that it will work.

The soundtrack now accompanies me every day. "Shabash, shabash," I whisper after tearing myself away from The Simpsons to write this sentence. "Shabash, shabash," as I watch my debate partner give a devastating speech. "Shabash, shabash," when Sarfraz does his trademark, borderline kamikaze shuffle down the pitch – against a bowler hurling it at over 90mph – and cheekily flicks the ball away for a boundary. Maybe he's saying this to himself as he does his thing, but I figure it can't hurt for someone to give him a little encouragement.

This is just one of many reasons I must watch this team. I must watch because knowing Pakistan are playing tonight is the biggest reason I got out of bed. I must watch because I illogically, secretly think I can influence the outcome by finding an online stream, observing every second of play, and putting my middle and index fingers to the right side of my head before each ball when Pakistan bat. I must watch because it feels essential to chant along with the crowd when they say *"Pakistan Zindabad!"* (long live Pakistan), and to send every bit of cosmic energy I possess to these men I've never met – with light brown faces, white uniforms and a language I don't know – fighting for something I believe I am also fighting for. I must watch because I really like saying *"Shabash, shabash"* and it would just feel weird now if I use it in my "real life" and don't say *"Shabash, shabash"* when Pakistan are actually playing.

Pakistan played cricket well before I was born, and they will, inshallah (God willing, another Urdu phrase that has snuck into my vocabulary), play cricket well after I die. Before Misbah, Afridi and Sarfraz, there were Imran, Wasim, Waqar, Mushy, Qadir, Javed, Inzy, and the greatest of them all, Hanif Mohammad. I have never watched these men do the thing they did – better than almost anyone in the world – in real time. All I can do is view hours and hours of YouTube highlights, research their stats, style and life story, watch and read all available English interviews, and check out a few Urdu interviews to see what (if anything) I can understand. I can admire the flair of Saeed Anwar, the grace of Zaheer Abbas (Zed), the deception of Saqlain, but I can't do much more than that. As for the men who will represent Pakistan cricket after I die, I have no doubt they will acquire fervent worshippers. They will cause divorces, make babies, cure the sick. Because they are Pakistan cricket players, all things will be possible – or so their fans will be led to believe.

• • •

When Pakistan are collapsing in a pathetic heap, wickets tumbling in a bumbling display of ineptitude, 3am is a melancholic time. When Pakistan are sprinting to victory, seizing control of the match with a chaotic blizzard of stump-shattering deliveries, 3am is a jubilant time. It's really that simple.

Or maybe not. Maybe time loses significance when I watch Pakistan cricket, and that phenomenon alone is significant. Maybe I am so desperate to engage that I jump on this excuse to shout and love and cry, and all those other things I gather most people do daily in their "real" lives. Or maybe I just want an escape from the drudgery, to dream and to be so fully immersed in another time and place and world, that residing there and forgetting about all the obligatory shit feels like it could be a permanent solution.

I don't think it would be fair, however, to equate dreaming with my obsessive fandom. Yes, I'm going to neglect sleep tonight when I watch Pakistan play Australia in a one-day game from around 10pm to 6am. But I don't believe watching that match will serve as a substitute for dreaming, even if it is comfortable, pleasant, and rejuvenating. The biggest difference is, if Pakistan win, I'll want to remember every detail, every humbled Australian player trudging off the ground, every beautiful in-swinging yorker, every delicious straight drive. I do not feel the same way about my dreams, most of which are vague, colourless, and filled with existential dread.

If I ever meet Misbah, I will not kiss his shirt, or bow down at his feet, or otherwise act like he's a god. I will not pinch myself to confirm I'm not dreaming. I'll just thank him (for being Misbah, though I doubt I'd have the courage to include that note), wish him luck, and continue with my life, as he will with his. The next time I take my hat off, I'll kiss the star – and his signature – and come to terms with the fact that my life now involves twice the kissing.

• • •

IT WAS 20 YEARS AGO TODAY

Two decades after his father Robert, the Archbishop of Canterbury, spoke at the Wisden dinner, James Runcie followed suit

Making a speech is like going out to bat. It brings back all those childhood memories of excitement, anticipation and dread – the opportunity to show off balanced by the possibility of abrupt humiliation.

My childhood was a mixture of three religions: Christianity, Music and, most important of all, Cricket.

My grandfather JWC Turner played for Worcestershire between 1911 and 1921, a career interrupted by the Great War and bookended by simultaneous success and failure. He made his happy debut, against Essex at Amblecote, in a crushing innings-and-228-run defeat – and scored his only century, 106, in his final game against Northamptonshire – a match Worcestershire lost by 356 runs. From early childhood, I was taught that cricket is, perhaps, the only game which can contain Kipling's twin impostors, triumph and disaster, at the same time.

My fondness for Worcestershire goes back to my grandfather teaching me how to hold my first cricket bat – and hearing about Tom Graveney's magisterial 165 against West Indies at The Oval in 1966. He was my boyhood hero, but I probably wouldn't go as far as Cardus when he wrote in *Wisden*: "If some destructive process were to eliminate all that we know about cricket, only Graveney surviving, we could reconstruct from him, from his way of batting and from the man himself, every outline of the game, every essential character and flavour which have contributed to cricket, the form of it, and its soul, and its power to inspire a wide and sometimes great literature."

I am sure Tom Graveney would have been amused and flattered at Cardus's assumption that he, alone, could provide the DNA of cricket – but the game has always inspired literary flights of fancy. Played in summer, at the height of the year, by sportsmen in their prime; each day becomes a metaphor for life that reaches full bloom and ends in shadow. Literature is the attempt to fix those fleeting moments, to describe the transient and the beautiful, and to make them endure on the page.

Thinking about cricket is often a matter of nostalgia brought short by statistics but – despite the sharp reality of the umpire's finger – I still cherish the April aroma of the first cut grass of spring, that brings back the memory of a new season and fresh hope – the smell of linseed oil, the first bruise of the ball after knocking in a Gray-Nicolls bat, finding the sweet spot that beckons the ball to give and go.

I think my life can be measured by watching great cricketing moments – from Graveney and D'Oliveira in the 1960s, right through to Stuart Broad's 8 for 15 against Australia and Johnny Bairstow's Test century against the South Africans, which still makes me cry just to think about it.

I read my first *Wisden* in 1967 when I was eight years old and the five cricketers of the year were a remarkable quintet: C Milburn, SM Nurse, BL D'Oliveira, JT Murray and RW Barber. Even then I wanted to be in it. I had promising beginnings: as a boy at prep school I was known as "Test Match Runcie" mainly due to my solid defence and inability to hit out. It was a question of being bullied really, of never having

the confidence to attack, of being scared of fast bowling – and because I wore spectacles.

Now, of course, it's possible to create an imaginary team that entirely consists of great spectacled cricketers. You could have Roy Marshall and Geoffrey Boycott opening the batting; a middle order of Zaheer Abbas, MJK Smith and Clive Lloyd with Eddie Barlow as the all-rounder. Paul Gibb could be the keeper, with two spinners – Alf Valentine and Daniel Vettori – and two quicks – Bill Bowes from England's Bodyline team and Devon Malcolm – with Hallam Moseley of Somerset as 12th man. All in specs!

But when I was young, I didn't think such things were possible. So, as the bowling got faster and the ball seemed to become harder and harder I took up tennis and moved from spectacles to spectator.

As a child, I watched as much as I could with my father – when I was 11, in 1970, he became Bishop of St Albans. He had just spent ten years running a theological college and so he not only knew the best students but also the ones who were best at cricket, and so perhaps it was a fluke – perhaps not – that the following year, the Diocese of St Albans won the *Church Times* cricket cup with a seven-wicket victory over Liverpool.

It was a long time before we could make the pilgrimage to Worcestershire, and when we finally did it was to see the Australians in 1993. There I met Johnners for the first time. He told a joke he had just heard and could barely contain his glee. It was about three football fans lost in the woods. They were starving but they managed to kill a deer. As they were roasting it over an open fire they discussed who was going to have the best meat. The first said: "I support Liverpool, so I'll have the liver." The second said: "I support Hearts, so I'll have the heart," and the third said: "I support Arsenal and I'm not very hungry." Johnners laughed as if it was the funniest thing he had ever heard.

Playing in that game was the young Shane Warne. It was a few weeks before the famous ball of the century to dismiss Mike Gatting – that ball came when I was making a film in Weston-super-Mare and the actor Jim Carter made us stop the filming as soon as he'd heard about it. There's priorities for you.

And, if you can measure a life by the games you have seen, you can also prepare for a death. When my father was diagnosed with cancer in 1997, I suggested we flew to the West Indies to watch the cricket, and so we went to Antigua for the sixth Test – a rain-interrupted game in which my dad used a gap in play to pop out and consecrate a bishop.

On the way over, we were upgraded by Continental Airlines. The flights involved an overnight stopover in New York and the following morning I realised that I had so enjoyed the in-flight hospitality that I had left all the tickets for the connecting flights on the plane. At the queue for the check-in the next morning, my father said: "You will have to deal with this," and so I went up to an attractive young woman at the counter and confessed all. She said it would be difficult. We would have to pay for the flights all

over again. And why were we going to Antigua?

"For the cricket," I said.

"The Test match?'

"That's right."

"Out of the West Indian bowling attack," she asked, "do you prefer Walsh or Ambrose?"

"Walsh, I think. I'd be more scared of Ambrose but I'd rather watch Walsh. He's got a lovely action and he plays with a smile on his face."

"I'll get you your tickets right away," she said. "I'm his cousin."

My father couldn't wait to tell the story when we got home – and I think he then claimed that this exchange had been his – because that's what we do – we turn our lives into narrative.

It was our last trip together, but we talked and talked. Watching cricket is the perfect disguise for difficult conversations. It allows us to imagine we are not talking to each other when we are. We can pretend we are not really saying all these difficult things about an impending death, the state of our marriage, looming bankruptcy or a terrible betrayal by a friend or employer – because we are looking ahead, "watching the cricket" – yet, of course, we are saying these things, but we are saying them while looking at something else, within the protection of a ground, a boundary, a world in which there will always be another day, alive with possibility, when everything can and will be different.

I remember my grandfather not only teaching me how to take guard but also telling me about how to walk out to bat; to look at the field of play and notice the gaps. Off side first – cut if it's short and wide, drive if it's on a length – remember the worst fielders are often at mid-off – then come back down the leg side. Take guard, call clearly, show your confidence, play each ball in turn, don't worry about what's past, stay alive to every opportunity. You had to notice everything.

It's the same in fiction. Henry James's advice to the would-be novelist is: "Try to be one of the people on whom nothing is lost". And in Thomas Hardy's poem "Afterwards", he writes that he would like to be remembered as "a man who used to notice such things."

Writers are often asked where they get their ideas from. Well, you could start by noticing the index of unusual occurrences from this year's *Wisden*: dog brings forward Test tea, illegal bat wins match, sun stops play, run out by a nose, first-class team declare at 24 for 7 on first morning, match abandoned after umpires fall simultaneously ill. All of these index headings make you want to look up the story behind them, or – in the best cricketing tradition, make one up instead.

In my detective series, *The Grantchester Mysteries*, I don't start so much with plot as with context. For example, I wanted to write about cricket in any case: but I particularly wanted to do so after I'd read a report about Hitler watching English prisoners of war playing the game and rejecting its take-up in Germany because he considered it "insufficiently violent".

I had an idea to write a crime story about the death of a finger-licking spinner who could be killed by poison applied to the seam of the ball. I had great difficulty working out how this could be done (how could you get the poison to stay on? how could it be re-applied between overs? would the umpires have to be involved?), and I think I would have benefited from the few additional props described by Derek Pringle in his essay on ball-tampering in this year's edition. I will never look on Murray Mints, Fishermen's Friends, and lip salve and sweat so innocently again.

Writers use cricket for context, simile and metaphor. You could argue that opening a conversation is the art of bowling a ball and seeing what comes back.

When I was 23 I went to mime school in Paris. I know. Unlikely, but true. One of the classes was on *le mélodrame*, the art of the melodramatic gesture. We were split into pairs and given a tennis ball. You had to throw the ball, underarm, between you and freeze your gesture. For example, I throw the ball while saying the line: "*Mon trésor,*" and freeze the gesture. My partner catches the ball, holds her gesture, looks at the precious ball and says to it: "*Mon amour.*"

Well, this went on for quite a long time. So I decided to spice things up a bit by bowling over-arm. A bit of a leg-break. "*Mon trésor.*"

Unfortunately my partner failed to read the flight of the ball – it was a disguised delivery out of the back of the hand – and dropped it. The teacher was unamused: "*Monsieur Jacques, Monsieur*

Jacques, vous ne trouverez jamais de jeune fille si vous jouez au cricket." ["Master Jack, Master Jack, you'll never find a girl if you play cricket."]

"Au contraire," I replied, *"c'est la seule chose dans la vie encore plus compliquée que l'amour."* ["On the contrary, it's the only thing in life more complicated than love."]

To which the French girl opposite replied, simply, and in English: "Prat."

But, in awkward situations, people often turn to the language of cricket. An entire adult life – or a bad best man's speech – can be described in cricketing cliché: you "bowl a maiden over" and then, on your wedding night, "after the covers come off," you "bring out the third man." But, after kids come along, you enter "the corridor of uncertainty," you try to "play with a straight bat" but "stray after a wide one when you should have left well alone," find yourself "on a sticky wicket" and "get caught." You're then "hit for six" in the divorce courts and "retire hurt" before walking up the steps "at close of play," having "had a good innings," to "the great long room in the sky."

But you don't find cricket writers writing in such a way – they have to sweat a bit more at their similes and metaphors. Writing, like cricket, is often hard graft. You have to find your own rhythm. It can be excruciatingly dull, you don't always know what you're doing or how it's going to turn out but, like cricket, it can all change utterly, in a moment, with an idea, a paragraph, a sentence or even a word – a single delivery.

You just have to stay on the field, keep your confidence up and when the men in white coats finally come to take you away, perhaps you should do so with the grace of the Hampshire batsman Henry Horton, whom John Arlott referred to as having "the ugliest stance, and the straightest bat, in English cricket."

Arlott wrote of Horton in his 1964 biographical note: "Find him in the dressing-room after he is out and you would never know whether he had made a duck or a hundred: he will be cleaning his bat, with the edge of a piece of broken glass, punctilious as a jeweller with a priceless piece of plate, removing every mark (though not that ineradicably deep dent in the middle of the 'meat'). You would not know whether he had made a duck or a hundred, true; but you *would* know if he had been run out."

A duck or a century – triumph or disaster – the important thing is to have been involved in the game, taken every opportunity, and have lived and noticed as much as you can.

You don't want to have led a "did not bat" kind of a life.

• • •

THE YOUNG ONES

*They say you never forget the first cricket game you watched
live. Here are a few who got an early taste.*

FATHER AND SONS
Imran Khan catches the action with Qasim and Sulaiman during the fourth one-day international
between Pakistan and England at the Rawalpindi Cricket Stadium in December 2005.
Photo: Paul Gilham/Getty Images

RIGHT
BABY'S DAY OUT:
Brad Haddin watches his son
Zac practise his wicket-keeping
skills during an Australia training
session at the MCG in December
2010.
Photo: Hamish Blair/Getty Images

BELOW
WHISTLE-BLOWER
A young boy cheers West Indies
on during a Test match against
Australia at Sabina Park, Jamaica
in May 2008.
*Photo: Timothy A Clary/AFP/Getty
Images*

ONCE UPON A TIME

A couple of boys and a dog join the crowd watching the day unfold on the village green at Oxted, Surrey in 1966.

Photo: Evening Standard/Getty Images

CATCHING 'EM YOUNG
A mother and child watch the New Zealand team practise at the Police Sports Club in Barbados, ahead of the 2007 World Cup.
Photo: Saeed Khan/AFP/Getty Images

ABOVE

FLAGGING IT UP

A Pakistani and a Sri Lankan watch the first day of the opening Test between their two countries at the Galle International Stadium in June 2012.

Photo: Ishara S Kodikara/AFP/Getty Images

BELOW

QUEERING THE PITCH

Excited schoolboys join the adults on the wicket at The Oval after Clive Lloyd makes a century in July 1973. Ray Illingworth (far-right, top) is protesting about possible damage to the pitch.

Photo: Leonard Burt/Central Press/Hulton Archive/Getty

THE ONE AND ONLIES

Lawrence Booth on the cricketers who played one first-class innings – and scored a hundred

One of them died last year. One died almost a century earlier, at the Second Battle of Bullecourt. Another became chief of staff of the United Nations' peace-keeping force in Cyprus. Yet another is a qualified surgeon. There are nine in all, and they share a geeky secret: each scored a hundred in his only first-class innings. Imagine buying one lottery ticket, ever – and winning. Is this how these men felt?

Cricket anoraks are familiar with the story of Andy Ganteaume, the West Indian whose Test career consisted of a single innings – 112 against England in Trinidad in 1947–48 – and who thus finished, uniquely, with a higher average than Bradman. But Ganteaume had the memory of 49 other first-class matches to sustain him into old age. The nine in this list had or have no such luxury. Or perhaps it didn't bother them: they dipped into a world beyond the reach of most, excelled instantly, then moved on to more pressing matters. Still, a hundred in your only innings: it's the kind of CV detail some of us would kill for.

This curiosity arose during a proofreading session for the new edition of *Wisden*. Kapil Seth, a seamer whose lone first-class innings yielded 125 not out from No.10 for Madhya Pradesh against Vidarbha at Indore during the 2000–01 Ranji Trophy, was making a premature appearance in obituaries, having been struck down at the age of 36 by hepatitis. Some bright spark – though not the editor – thought it would be a good idea to embellish his entry with a table detailing the other eight. So here we are.

Morbidly, Seth swung the balance: a slim majority – five of the nine – are now dead. The other four were dimly aware they had done something special, but had no real sense of their exclusivity. (And who can blame them: they have a life to lead, after all.)

Shahbaz Bashir (102 for the Netherlands against the UAE in an Intercontinental Cup match at Deventer in 2012) laughed heartily on hearing the news. Avinash Sharma (185 not out for Oxford against Cambridge in the Parks in 2010) knew he had broken some kind of Varsity match record, but didn't know much more. Stuart Moffat (169 for Cambridge against Oxford, also in the Parks, in 2002) wanted to know the identity of his confreres.

And Suresh Harding (100 not out for Sinhalese Sports Club against Burgher Recreation Club in Colombo in 1988–89) was intrigued to know how I had tracked down his number. In each case, our chat was a delight.

As much as anything, the list attests to the strangeness of cricket's parameters. One man's first-class match is another's food and drink. Three of the games involved Oxford University, and two involved Tasmania in the days before they were allowed into the Sheffield Shield. If Seth appears to be the most harshly treated – he was immediately dropped because he failed to take a wicket in four overs – then Norman Callaway is the most poignant.

For one thing, Callaway was playing in a game that was high-class as well as first-class: New South Wales against Queensland at Sydney in 1914–15. He came in at 17 for three, moved to a half-century in an hour, and – only half an hour after that – to a century with a straight six. He finished with 207, and New South Wales won by an innings. Then the war intervened. The Allies were desperate to break the Hindenburg Line on the Western Front, and finally did so in September 1918. But it was a costly obsession: Callaway was among the dead. It seems right that he is the only double-centurion in the list – and inconceivable that his record will ever be broken.

Stanley Wootton survived the war, and later played Australian rules for South Melbourne and Richmond. But he also got a game for the Victorian cricket team, who occasionally deigned to take on the upstart islanders of Tasmania. In that game, in 1923–24, Wootton kept wicket, pulled off two stumpings and, batting at No.7, top-scored with 105 in 90 minutes

out of a total of 256. On 97, he was hit on the body; the blow meant Wootton didn't take part in Victoria's successful second-innings run chase. According to Ray Webster's First-Class Cricket in Australia, "Wootton remained unwell for some time after returning to Melbourne". And that, as far as his first-class career was concerned, was that: unscathed by bullets, invalided by a cricket ball.

Twelve seasons later, Horace Grangel became another beneficiary of Victoria's largesse towards the Tasmanians. He made 108, and Tasmania lost by an innings. Still, Grangel did get to make his debut alongside Bill Baker, who later ticked off an even quirkier stat by becoming the only man to stump Bradman twice in the same game. Inevitably perhaps, we digress.

So far, so Australian. But in 1938 at Camberley in Surrey, Michael Harbottle put a stop to that. Playing for the Army against Oxford, Harbottle scored 156 before being dismissed by Desmond Eagar, the future Hampshire captain and father of Patrick, cricket's greatest photographer. He rose to the rank of Brigadier, spent time in Aden, Cyprus and Sierra Leone, and – improbably, you might think – became general secretary of the World Disarmament Campaign. And all because the Navy were said to have rejected him because of his bunions.

And so to the four who are still with us. The first I track down, Shahbaz Bashir, has ambitions of erasing his name from the list altogether, so it's best we deal with him quickly before he gets the chance. A Pakistani immigrant in Amsterdam, Bashir qualified for the Netherlands in 2012, and was chosen for the four-day game against the UAE after the Dutch captain

Peter Borren picked up an injury. He talks now with the kind of casual confidence only an unretired cricketer can muster:

"The most important thing for me was that I'd played with about 10 of the guys in the UAE team during my time in Pakistan, and I'd played with their coach," he says. "I felt ready. There was no pressure. For me, it was an easy experience. There was a lot of rain during the game, so it became all about my batting. But I also bowled nine overs, seven maidens, one for five."

He remembers it as if it was yesterday. "Peter Borren said that if he returned, he'd be back, so I spent the next three years waiting for Peter Borren to be injured again. If you ask me, it was lucky for them that I played. I'd played a lot in the Topklasse cricket in Holland, and was top scorer in the year Neil McKenzie, the South African Test batsman, played. In 2014, I was player of the year in Holland. I thought, maybe they can use me better. Dropping me was not really an answer to a batsman who had made 100. I've been far better than some of the players in the team. But I'm not going to ask them. I will play if they come to me." Bashir is 33, and hasn't given up hope. Despite it all, he sounds upbeat, not bitter.

Avinash Sharma, a New Zealander, won a scholarship to Oxford to study for a Masters in public health. Three weeks before the Varsity match that earned him his small chunk of immortality, he was fielding close to the wicket against the Durham Academy when a fierce sweep from his fellow Kiwi Tom Latham – now a Test opener – connected with his ankle. He was in pain, but determined to win his Blue: the physician was not quite ready to heal himself. Only after he had taken Cambridge to the cleaners did he visit

the John Radcliffe hospital: the ankle was broken. He was in plaster for six weeks, and finally returned to New Zealand to qualify as a surgeon.

He carried on playing cricket, helping Cornwall CC in Auckland – once home to the Crowe brothers and Mark Greatbatch – win the national club championship. But surgery was his thing. Did he ever think about adding to his first-class experience? Sharma is calm, considered and sanguine; he sounds like a man you'd trust with a scalpel: "It's often a debate we have. If I hadn't wanted to pursue surgery, I'd maybe have had a go. I just saw it as an opportunity to make my mark. I didn't really think about scoring a century. I just wanted to help us beat the Tabs [Oxford students' nickname for Cambridge], especially because we'd just lost the one-day game, when I'd made 51 at Lord's. It would have been great to have scored a hundred there…"

Sharma, now 35, lives in New York these days, where he is seeking a medical fellowship. But cricket remains a passion, and he plays for the Galacticos club in the Bronx. When we talk, he has just returned from a pre-season tour to Jamaica. Some guys have all the fun. Or so I thought, until I talked to Stuart Moffat. Eight years before Sharma butchered Cambridge, Moffat butchered Oxford. And a few months after he butchered Oxford, he was scoring a try for Scotland against Romania at Murrayfield. "I was born in the wrong era," he says. "I'd have been a good amateur in both sports. But I didn't love being a professional rugby player, and it would probably have been the same with cricket. When doing something you love turns into a job… it becomes regimented, there are dietary requirements, lots of travelling, living in hotel rooms... it's not the glamorous life some people think."

Moffat, who runs a property investment and management company in Edinburgh, won four rugby caps, including a famous win over the Springboks. He modestly portrays himself as a dabbler, which is often the way of those who don't quite realise how talented they are. When he arrived at Cambridge to study management, he was reassessing his relationship with rugby after breaking his leg in his final year at Loughborough. Cambridge's cricket coach, Chris Scott, asked the university's rugby club if they had any budding cricketers. Moffat volunteered, along with Mark Chapman-Smith, a New Zealander. Chapman-Smith played in the one-day Varsity match at Lord's, where Moffat was 12th man, but then fell injured before the four-day game in the Parks. Moffat took his place and hit 169 as Cambridge racked up a Varsity record 604. A fortnight later, he embarked on a professional rugby career with Glasgow Caledonians. A few months after that, it was Romania in front of nearly 35,000 at Murrayfield.

"People ask me a lot about the one-off innings," he says. "It's a strange one. Cricket was always my first love – I was serious about it before rugby. I'd grown up playing on Scottish pitches, which were a seamer's paradise, so the surfaces in Cambridge felt like concrete. I guess the stars aligned and I hit a vein of form. But rugby had just gone professional at the time, and I hadn't planned to play much cricket at Cambridge anyway. In terms of rugby, I never felt I fulfilled my potential. And a hundred in the Varsity match isn't exactly an international hundred. But I was delighted to be involved." Moffat is 39, with three kids under the age of five.

His sporting days are behind him, but the memories live on.

Suresh Harding's memories have been helpfully preserved in black and white. His mother kept the newspaper cuttings of his hundred in Colombo, and he's reading out the reports down the phone from his home in Melbourne. Like Bashir, Sharma and Moffat, Harding is tickled to be told he's part of a special gang, and still grateful, after all these years, that the Burgher captain chose to bowl first on a relaid surface. "He made a big mistake," chuckles Harding, who put on 142 with Aruna Gunawardene (who went on to play a single one-day international for Sri Lanka), and an unbroken 112 with Asanka Gurusinha, a seasoned Test batsman. "I was on 98 when Gurusinha overtook me, despite batting a place below me at No.4. So I was almost the first person to score a hundred on the new pitch."

As so often, injury changed the story. Harding opened the bowling, but was cramping badly and pulled a hamstring. It ruled him out for eight weeks. In the meantime, an opportunity arose for a three-month break in Australia from his job with Lipton's tea. He enjoyed the lifestyle, and eventually returned for good. "And 28 years later, I'm still here," he says.

Was he disappointed not to have played another first-class game? "Of course I was. When I briefly went back to Sri Lanka in 1990, I played a few tier-two games. I think I'd have played a bit more if I'd not returned to Australia. But it's nice to know I'm part of this list. I got a shock when you texted me. I showed my friend and we both started laughing."

Well, you would, wouldn't you.

• • •

Celebrating

the **best** of cricket, the **worst** of **cricket** and **everything** in **between**

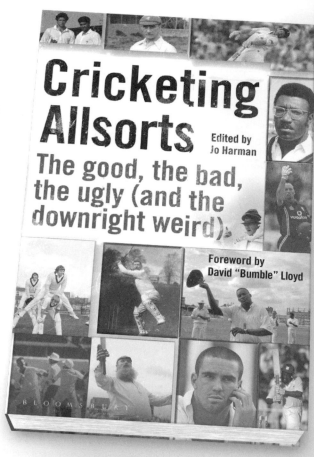

Cricketing Allsorts

Edited by Jo Harman

The good, the bad, the ugly (and the downright weird)

Foreword by David "Bumble" Lloyd

BLOOMSBURY

Unusual captains | Bowling partnerships | Hysterical overreactions | Unlikeliest fans | Memorable sixes | The new Bothams | Brazen product endorsements | Remarkable journeys

www.wisden.com

ON DISCOVERING
DEREK BIRLEY

Tim Cooke is thrilled by a cricket writer after his own heart

I'd not heard of Derek Birley until Saturday, 4 June last year. I can be so precise about the date because I was on my way to watch the usually taciturn American author Don DeLillo discuss his latest novel, *Zero K* – a cold and philosophical depiction of a cryonics lab buried somewhere beneath the border of Uzbekistan – at the Southbank Centre in London. It was the first of two live interviews with him I was attending that week, and I'd trekked five hot miles from my home in Hackney for it, shooting pictures of classic cars, cormorants and clouds of charcoal smoke as I went. I was ambling along the final stretch of the Thames, with a to-be-signed first edition copy of *White Noise* in my backpack, when the familiar arrangement of weekend bookstalls inevitably drew me off course.

Shielded from the heat beneath the first arch of Waterloo Bridge, I browsed the stockpile. I fondled collectible copies of *Jeeves and Wooster* and considered an expensive boxed set of Proust's *Remembrance of Things Past*, before flicking through Hermione Hobhouse's *Lost London*, an architectural history of the city. I strolled past piles of cookery books and assortments of maps on display and, at the end of a long row of folding tables, turned left, running my fingertips over a series of smooth dustcovers. In between a pair of scuffed-up football annuals, I spotted a small beige and orange text, antique-looking and decorated with an image of a batsman wearing what could be misconstrued as the colours of the MCC.

The picture, I later learned, was a caricature of Lord Hawke that first appeared in *Vanity Fair* in 1892, accompanied by the caption "Yorkshire Cricket" – definitely not the MCC, then. The book was Birley's *The Willow Wand*, a rebellious debunking of the great myths of the game – primarily concerned with discussing the establishment's sententious claims at chivalry, fair

play and other such self-aggrandising elevations. The phrase "not cricket", for example, comes in for considerable flak, as does the old feudal vision and the bucolic ideal – the sport as anachronism. The author's approach was one after my own heart: he treated the game as something great and complex, but not the poetic exercise of moral decorum it has been pompously, and often falsely, described as over the years.

Having purchased a good number of rewarding sport books in similarly impulsive fashion, I paid three pounds and popped it, along with Hobhouse's work, in my backpack. Pleased, I shuffled out from the shadows and made for the Southbank Centre's balcony bar, where I watched tourists snap sun-drenched London from the crowded decks of large riverboats.

Over the next few days, *The Willow Wand* slipped in amongst a pile of unread books in my living room and remained there until the time came to think about my next article for *The Nightwatchman*. Because of its subtitle, "Some cricket myths explored," I naively assumed it to be about an obscure and fantastical cricketing mythology, perhaps concerned with elves and ogres, but more likely to do with dressing-room legends of absurd wagers and local brawls, 30-ball overs and countless cow-corner sixes in a row – that kind of thing. I was totally wrong.

One morning, as winter fell, I unearthed the book from my collection and took it with me on a short saunter along the Regent's Canal, from Victoria Park to King's Cross and on to the British Library. I was hoping that a quick scan of its early chapters might spark

an idea worth pursuing – a tall tale with mysterious origins to investigate, perhaps. I settled on a green bench, surrounded by the sounds of the cold city, and watched a globule of oil, iridescent and sinister, float between two slices of soaking white bread. Fighting the urge to rejoin David Mummery and the wildly entertaining supernatural flâneur Josef Kiss in Michael Moorcock's *Mother London*, I began *The Willow Wand* in earnest.

As well as its progressive, almost radical, spirit, I particularly enjoyed Birley's free approach to criticism. He took no prisoners, with few of his predecessors avoiding harsh, often comic denunciation; Neville Cardus, among many others, gets a good kicking. But Birley's well-supported disdain reaches far beyond his own field and into the arena populated by some of the game's most celebrated historical figures, with WG Grace – whenever I read his initials, I can't help but hope "Sebald" will follow – and Lord Hawke caught in the crossfire. He wrote scathingly of Hawke that his "autobiography must rank amongst the least modest books ever put together."

Just as I was reading these lines, a commotion in the sparse foliage overhead – two or three chaffinches, I thought – alerted me to a figure approaching. A middle-aged man of medium build was striding towards me. He was wearing a blue waterproof coat, with a clipboard resting across his left forearm; I thought he might be an employee of the Canal and River Trust, but I couldn't be sure. As he came closer, I noticed a front tooth was missing. His cheeks were pink and lined with purple and red veins, and his smile rigid and fulsome. A wiry track of light-brown hair ran halfway around his otherwise bald head.

He began our conversation by asking if I'd heard about the live grenade found at the bottom of the canal near Mile End station. "They get all sorts down there," he explained, with a northern twang I couldn't quite place. "You wouldn't believe me if I told you..." He didn't tell me, for on noticing Birley's book, he almost burst with excitement. "Wonderful!" he exclaimed. "I read it when I was a lad and then again a few years back. What do you make of it?" I'd only just started so had little to offer, but we talked for a while about the old social divisions in cricket – north and south, the player and the gentleman, amateur versus professional – before he sighed: "Ah well, best get on." He left without ever mentioning the official business that had apparently brought us together.

So, as it turned out, Birley was far better known than I'd initially, and rather ignorantly, assumed. On returning to my flat, I tapped his name into Google and found that as well as publishing *The Willow Wand* in 1979, he'd penned three volumes in the 1990s on the history of British sport. His last book, *A Social History of English Cricket*, published in 1999, won both the Cricket Society's Book of the Year and the William Hill Sports Book of the Year – more a household name, then, than a forgotten mystery.

As spring rose, I found myself reading that revered social history in short bursts on my bus commute to the school I teach at in Newham, and to a nursery near the Olympic Park, where for one week I was learning about the principles of forest education. On an empty top deck, bathed in early-morning light, I slipped back in time to feudal England, where the nature and form of leisure and competition were inextricably linked to class and politics. I read of the game's origins in pubs, booze and gambling; of blood sports, land enclosures, Oliver Cromwell and the Restoration; of breaking the Sabbath and the effect of the Industrial Revolution; of the Golden Age. Birley's references to the "dream-world of cricket" seemed fitting, as on one occasion, I recall, I drifted into a deep dream of my own, a fugue state on route 425.

A brief summary of Birley's exceptional life, which ended in 2002, goes someway to explaining his flair with prose and my enthusiasm for his writing. He was born in West Yorkshire in 1926 and raised in a mining community, amid the county's cricketing heartland. Whether or not he'd have described it as peppered with "dark satanic mills", I can't say – he seemed to detest stereotypes. After a short military career, most of which was spent serving as an interpreter in the Russian sector of post-war Berlin, he studied English literature at Queen's College, Cambridge, where he won a prestigious short story competition, sharing the top prize with JG Ballard, no less.

You'd be forgiven for guessing that Birley's professional career was based in the arts, but he was in fact a dedicated educationalist, becoming a teacher and then administrator, with a hand – perhaps only slight – in the emergence of the polytechnic, and seven successful years as vice chancellor at the University of Ulster. His tenure included a controversial but pioneering merger, and the introduction of an increased array of courses designed to meet the diverse needs of prospective students. Known to deplore any form of discrimination, he also fought hard for the educational rights of women and minority groups. It's little surprise he was awarded a knighthood in recognition of his long and illustrious career.

While I can't find any footage to give physical character to his achievements, Don McCloy, in his *Guardian* obituary, described him as charismatic and formidable, with "a Yorkshire grit as abrasive as the Northern Ireland variety".

The majority of Birley's writing about sport – which seems, in comparison to his main line of work, to have been little more than a hobby – came during the twilight of his life. His style was at once spiky, amusing and scholarly, with the occasional hint of poetry, which must surely have arisen from his love of literature. His books contain plenty of astute and enjoyable references to literary figures, about many of whom he was clearly passionate: there's William Blake, Lewis Carroll, Homer, and myriad more. He once told the *Independent* that he preferred plays and poetry to prose, and that he absolutely adored Shakespeare. Combine all this with his tangled appreciation of the game and you have the ingredients for a seriously interesting take on cricket.

With Birley, I share a love a literature, a varied career in education – I worked behind the scenes in FE, before retraining as a teacher – and an intense urge to write about the things that interest me most; plus, I was raised in an industrial South Wales town, where the cricket experience is far more relatable to that of the north than south of England. I also share his belief, expressed beautifully in *The Willow Wand*, that sports can be "measured according to the satisfactions they offer individuals, or according to how they help individuals cope with life," but they are "likely to suffer... if a society chooses them to achieve specific social or political purposes". He continued: "Nor is the society itself likely to benefit for long."

It's always a joy coming upon great men and women in unexpected places, with ideas that inspire and invigorate. Birley's democratic, down-to-earth, unvarnished, nostalgia-light approach to the game speaks to me of considerably more than just cricket, but that's for another time. His promotion of access and opportunity, which was a priority in both his educational and sporting careers, is laudable; it's a mentality that brings vibrancy and a diversity of voices to our sport. It's also one that allows for such fortuitous discoveries as mine – providing countless delights, as well as validation and form to some unexplored frustrations – on a hot summer's day in London, strolling along the South Bank.

. . .

BODI OF EVIDENCE

Luke Alfred and Tristan Holme lift the lid on match-fixing

Hardly anyone remembers Gulam Bodi anymore; he's just a sad case of roadkill on cricket's superhighway. Truth be told, Bodi doesn't remember himself very much, what he did, where he went, what it felt like. He used to bat with his shirt off in the Wanderers nets, fending off throw-downs from Geoff Toyana or Gordon Parsons, the Lions coaches. Later, there'd be a spell from teammate Pumi Matshikwe or, if he was unlucky, from the always-mean Hardus Viljoen. There was always banter, casual camaraderie, common purpose. On most days Neil McKenzie would be giving him lip or playing the fool, or both. It was strangely comforting, this world. Now they're images from a different life, one Bodi knows he had but can't quite get a grip on.

"So how are you," we ask in mid-January 2017, just over 12 months after Bodi was banned from all cricket and cricket-related activities for 20 years, with five suspended.

"No, I'm alright, I'm alright. You've got to move on."

It's a peculiarly South African trait – answering in the affirmative yet starting with a negative – and it means all kinds of things, some self-evident, some more elusive. But hand it to the man, move on he has. After dabbling in potatoes, cosmetics and used cars, Bodi and a mate entered the motor-oil business. "A big deal is in the pipeline," he told us without a trace of humour in the months prior to the deal's conclusion. Now that matters have moved from the refinery, along the proverbial pipeline and into a warehouse, Bodi says they're looking for distributors, garages and car workshops. They have, he says, to get a foothold in the market.

As he chats about his plans for the business he manages to sound hopeful without really being hopeful at all, and then, as if remembering something, he stops abruptly – he can't say any more, his lawyers have advised him that he shouldn't be talking to the press.

When Bodi isn't scrambling to make a buck and trying to remember what

it was like playing cricket, he's out on his road bike, going on long rides with a group of his mates. "Mainly on the weekends around Krugersdorp on the West Rand," he says. "We're looking at maybe 30-kilometre rides with the guys."

Bodi's deepest love, though, is fishing – his therapy and his worship. Sometimes he fishes off the banks of the Vaal River, the muddy-brown that winds its way west across the country before reaching the Orange and disgorging into the Atlantic. Fishing at the Vaal is strictly "catch-and release" stuff, sometimes with his old Titans' teammate Ethy Mbhalati, sometimes with pals he has managed to pick up along the way.

The bank of the Vaal was one of the locations where Bodi first started toying with the idea of match-fixing in the 2015–16 RAM SLAM Challenge, South Africa's domestic T20 competition. There's time to think as you bait your hook, opportunity to ponder as you cast into the great swirl. As he fished for carp and barbel later in February and March 2015, Bodi saw the looming thunderheads. Contracting took place in April, a couple of months away, and, on the balance of probabilities, his was unlikely to be renewed.

He was in his late thirties, had always been a bits-and-pieces man, and his routine no longer had any lustre. For the son of Indian shopkeeper parents who emigrated from the state of Gujarat 30-odd years ago, Bodi certainly hadn't done badly. The only son in a family of girls, he learned to play in a ramshackle town about 50 kilometres west of Johannesburg

called Azaadville. As a cricketer he was always hardworking in the nets, although no great achiever on the "bleep" test. Despite his humble upbringing (Azaadville feels like a small town in northern India or Pakistan), Bodi could be almost touchily proud of where he came from. He was certainly no "development player", although, given the cul-de-sac in which he found himself, categories were fast becoming redundant. He didn't want to think about being without a job, so he sometimes went fishing with Viljoen and Quinton de Kock at Inchanga near Umgeni, north of Durban on the KwaZulu-Natal coast. "There it's deep-sea game fishing. Proper stuff. Hardus and I went out and Quinton came along a couple of times as well."

Up at Inchanga he tried to forget but in trying to forget he ended up thinking about his future. He was part of the first generation of young, newly professionalised South African cricketers in the late 1990s, playing for SA under-19s in 1998 alongside Michael Lumb, Grant Elliott and Morne van Wyk, and a post-school qualification was never on the cards. Cricket was neither a lifestyle nor a crutch: it was Bodi's entire world. Without it, he had not even the slightest idea of what to do.

He'd casually frittered away what he had earned, including some good paydays with the Delhi Daredevils in 2012 and with the Lions in the CLT20 later that same year. They got to the final at the Wanderers, losing to the Sydney Sixers, but the money had already slipped through his hands. A penchant for gambling didn't help.

While he fished with Mbhalati in the months that followed (as he suspected, his contract at the Lions wasn't renewed), the outline of a plan began to take shape. He knew some people who knew some people. He realised that much of the RAM SLAM T20 – 27 matches in all – would be shown live on Indian television. Towards the end of the South African winter of 2015, he started hanging around Willowmoore Park in Benoni, the venue for several matches in the Africa T20 Cup (a pre-season tournament featuring Zimbabwe, Namibia and some smaller unions) due to be played that September.

There he courted people, renewing old friendships, baiting his hook. In some cases he met players in parking lots; on other occasions the preferred hang-out was at upmarket Johannesburg strip joints with fixers. The ultimate aim of the meetings was the same: to hide behind his jokey, often charmingly incompetent persona to establish if the person being spoken to was prepared to corrupt the integrity of the T20 matches in which they would later play. In a haphazard, make-it-up-as-you-go-along kind of way, Bodi's plan was coming together.

But as September collapsed into the summer proper of October and November, Bodi began to see his initiatives take on a life of their own. Some players who he'd either approached (Symes) or fished with (Mbhalati) weren't going to play T20 for their respective franchises. He needed someone closer to the action, a skipper capable of changing the batting order on a whim, or of rationalising weird decisions. He reached out to Thami Tsolekile, the Lions captain. He and Tsolekile met bookies at Rivonia strip club in mid-September 2015, shortly before the start of the season. Bodi didn't stay past midnight because his dad was desperately ill and he was called away with his father dying a couple of days later.

At the time it struck him that he hadn't strategised carefully enough: in reaching out to Tsolekile, who in turn made players close to him – like Lonwabo Tsotsobe and Alviro Petersen – aware of what was going on, he lost control of his plan. Here was a match-fixing caper in which the go-between had written himself out of his script. Bodi realised that his role in the whole messy enterprise was becoming more and more negligible, a feeling confirmed when the fixers didn't even bother to return his increasingly agitated calls.

• • •

Fishing of an altogether different proposition took place throughout 2016 by David Becker, the independent lawyer contracted by Cricket South Africa (CSA) to lead the Anti-Corruption Unit's (ACU) match-fixing investigations. Becker – a careful, relentless man – doggedly circled around his suspects. It sometimes seemed as though the investigation was going nowhere (six months elapsed between Bodi's suspension and CSA's next announcement on the matter) but, inevitably, names were pulled like fish from the waves.

The fact that Bodi changed his testimony three times didn't help;

he also changed lawyers within the same firm. Initially he hoped the ACU's enquiries would go away, before reluctantly co-operating. Finally, under the influence of his new counsel, he became more circumspect in his willingness to share information. The other players named by Bodi and suspected by the authorities initially denied any wrongdoing, forcing Becker to painstakingly sift through cell-phone records and Uber manifests. He tried to recover CCTV footage; screen-grabs of potential bookies' cell phones were added to the mix. He and his chief investigator, Louis Cole, needed to cold-heartedly trap players in their own omissions, their own lies, with the early leads often coming from Bodi. They had to decipher the coded language the players used in text messages, a strange Esperanto in which "Indian gent happy to make big donation to your academy" was a common refrain.

If lack of cooperation wasn't enough, Tsolekile disappeared into the townships of the Western Cape under the guise of recovering from an Achilles injury. Jean Symes, another former Lions' teammate, denied he was in any way involved; Matshikwe hoped it would all go away. Mbhalati looked his chief executive at the Titans in the eye and swore nothing was wrong, although he was known to have a host of monthly garnishee orders that crippled him financially.

Becker didn't slacken, although months went by when no apparent progress was being made. Eventually, in mid-2016, Tsolekile, Mbhalati, Symes and Matshikwe were suspended from cricket for periods ranging from seven to 12 years. A former cricket official who preferred to remain anonymous said: "Pumi [Matshikwe] surprised me most. He was more the guy who would swan off to Sandton City to go and have a latte with McKenzie. He wasn't much of a clubber. The others were rough diamonds. They all loved to jol, to dabble and razzle and all that shit. Everyone always used to say that Pumi was a black guy in a white man's body but the others liked a party and a toot. Whether discipline was an issue at the Lions or not at the time one can't say for sure."

One man in all of this was never prepared to be put on the defensive by Becker's nagging line and length. Alviro Petersen, the former Proteas' opening batsman, insisted through 2016 that he was simply the whistle-blower, and took to social media to distance himself from the matter, insisting on his innocence. Becker and his investigative team knew better, suspecting that Petersen's argument didn't stack up. In late October, Petersen, through his lawyer Robin Twaddle, rejected an ACU plea bargain. Behind the scenes, however, he was known to be vacillating. Bodi always maintained that Petersen was more heavily involved than he claimed, despite Petersen's testimony to the contrary. When asked to comment on Petersen's two-year ban handed out in December 2016, he was non-committal. "That's got nothing to do with me now," he said. "I'm just not involved."

So distant has cricket become from Bodi's life nowadays that he speaks with no authority or interest about the Sri Lankan visit to South Africa, of which he watched precious little. Recently, though, he bought his three-year-old son Yusuf a rubber bat and ball. They play in the Azaadville yard. Yusuf has taken to batting left-handed like his dad, while Ahmed is still too small to pick up a bat – he's only eight months old.

As Bodi – a man who started off as a cricketer and finished off as a clown – gently tosses the ball to his son, he reflects on what might have been. In May 2002 he was once chosen for South Africa and was on the cusp of jetting to the Caribbean from the north of England, where he was bowling in freezing conditions for Leyland in the North Lancashire League. But in the first game of the season – muddy, two-jersey weather – Bodi broke the pinkie of his left hand while attempting a caught-and-bowled he failed to take.

Instead of flying from early-summer cold to the tour of a lifetime (Paul Adams, the Test incumbent, had already flown home and Boje had injured tendons in his shoulder, so there was a chance Bodi might actually play), he flew back to South Africa. His ticket to the sacred garden had been cruelly snatched away.

He'll show you the offending finger, if you ask. It's crocked and looks almost slightly deformed. After staring at the finger, you notice the hands. They're small, by any standards, certainly not Graeme Smith's beer kegs or Simon Harmer's bear-like paws. And they're stubby. You wonder in passing how Bodi could have been a wrist-spinner at all.

In the seasons that followed – as Bodi moved in a wide domestic arc from the Lions to the Dolphins to the Titans and back to the Lions – he bowled less

and less. He need to reinvent himself and played not only the pinch-hitter role and the opener role, but various roles down the order too.

Here was a cricketer whose contribution was not only difficult to weigh as he grew older, but one who was difficult to appreciate. What was he? He certainly wasn't what he started out as. What exactly did he have to offer and could what he offered be done as well if not better by someone else?

So increasingly as his career progressed, Bodi presented himself as the joker, the floater, the wise-ass, the clown, a better-developed corrective to his increasingly indistinct role as a cricketer. Dave Nosworthy, his coach for several seasons at the Titans, tells a story of Bodi waltzing into the Titans dressing-room and announcing that he could get a good deal on iPads at R500 a pop. The team's response was part intrigue, part incredulity, the more suspiciously inclined asking if they'd dropped off a truck. Bodi wasn't deterred. He duly came back the next day having visited the chemist, his arm full of eye-patches, the kind used by trans-Atlantic travellers flying business class. "Here are those eye-pads you ordered, boys," he announced with a chuckle.

• • •

The 2015-16 RAM SLAM started with a Newlands double-header one Friday night in late October, with the third match of the competition taking place upcountry that same day. The match the following Wednesday, however, between the Dolphins and the Lions at Kingsmead, has attracted subsequent attention because Bodi has told us on more than one occasion that the clash was only "hours away" from being fixed.

Quite what transpired in the Lions dressing-room that day has never been publically revealed. Bodi wasn't there. But his old mate Petersen certainly was; so were Tsolekile and Lonwabo Tsotsobe, who was sanctioned in late April 2017 on four charges by CSA, the most serious of which relates to "contriving to fix or to improperly influences matches". At the time of going to press, he had yet to formally respond to the charges. If Petersen is to be believed, he blew the whistle at about this time, having run with the process not because he conspired to fix matches but because he wanted to find out as much as possible about his teammates' deviance. Bodi rejects this wholeheartedly, as does Tsolekile, who Petersen publically threatened to sue if he divulged more of what he knows. Tsolekile should know the truth: he was in the most important position of all, with a captain's influence over the Lions' batting and bowling orders, who would bowl at the death and who would change ends.

Here we enter an echo chamber, with competing voices (and versions) bouncing off the walls, something that has proved particularly challenging for Becker, Cole and the ACU's small team of investigators. We know for certain that the Dolphins scored 174 for 6 with Kevin Pietersen scoring a 66-ball 115, this after they had stuttered to 68 for 4 in the 11th over; in reply, the Lions fell short by one run, with Dwaine Pretorius and Petersen the not-out batsmen on 17

and 48 respectively. They were only two wickets down.

While we can't pin down with absolute certainty what did or didn't happen at Kingsmead, we do know that when the Lions played the Titans in Potch two days later, a suspicious gentleman was removed from the grounds. The father of one of the Lions took a photograph of the said individual's cell-phone screen and it showed an illegal betting platform not available in South Africa. The players and authorities have argued that this match, like the Dolphins match 48 hours earlier, remained unaffected, although Heinrich Strydom – the chief executive of North West Cricket and therefore the man in charge of the ground – to this day knows nothing about the spectator's eviction.

Later that day CSA issued a press release, making the cricket community aware that suspected illegal betting syndicates had targeted the RAM SLAM. The press release gave rise to a year of ACU investigation, often tiresome work in the face of evasion and outright fraud from certain players. Bodi told the press a couple of months later that his "life had come to a standstill". He still lives in that twilight, frozen in time as history's bumbler, match-fixing's very own Mr Bean. Here was a cricketer whose mouth and brain were seldom in alignment, a personality trait that cost him dearly.

One former teammate said: "We were playing in a four-day Jukskei Derby [Bodi playing for the Titans against the Lions] and it was getting heated. There was some lip from Lions bowler, Friedel de Wet, which isn't really Friedel's style. He got so under Gulam's skin that Gulam walked down the pitch and said: 'Carry on and I'll f***en shoot you.' It created a bit of a stink and Shahid Wadvalla, the umpire, had to call him into the umpire's room afterwards. That was Gulam for you. But to be fair, while he said some idiot things, he was a hard-nosed cricketer. He always fronted up to mistakes. It was when the strong characters disappeared from around him that he struggled because he was impressionable. I often wonder what the death of his poor dad meant."

So ends Bodi's story – brazen, colourful, oddly touching, a clumsy footnote waiting for a chapter of the game that is yet to be written.

• • •

RETHINKING THE PANTHEON

Jaideep Varma takes stock of India's batting legends

First, an explainer: Impact Index is a holistic statistical system in cricket, whose fundamentals are centred around match context and series/ tournament context. It calculates everything from the scorecard and sniffs out details that may not be obvious to the naked eye. To start with, the system evaluates every single performance in a match only within the context of that game (as a ratio against the other 21 performances in the same match). Then, it looks at that performance from a series/ tournament perspective. When it is a high-impact performance, it increases in value (proportionate to the player's performances in that event and how his team eventually fares). This essential accounting for what goes on in the middle sifts out the real team players, making us rethink cricket history.

In Indian cricket's 85-year-long history, three men stand tall for their longevity, volume of runs and batting average: Sachin Tendulkar, Rahul Dravid and Sunil Gavaskar. The trio is head and shoulders above the rest, followed by VVS Laxman and Virender Sehwag – the former with the most memorable innings in Indian history, the latter with the biggest ones.

If you consider pure averages, Virat Kohli features high on the list among batsmen who have played over 50 Tests (the minimum criterion for this piece). Considerably behind Kohli are Mohammad Azharuddin, Mohinder Amarnath, Polly Umrigar, Sourav Ganguly, Dilip Vengsarkar, Navjot Sidhu, Gundappa Viswanath and Gautam Gambhir (in that order). Just shy of 50 Tests (48 to be precise), Cheteshwar Pujara will soon be an inevitable entrant on this list – though at a much higher average than Azharuddin's 45.03 – so we must mention him too.

These judgments can be made by anyone, based on the averages and aggregates system, the practice

of which has left cricket lolling imperviously in the middle of the last century. It leaves little room for nuance and context, resulting in several important stories never getting told. For instance, GR Viswanath and Chandu Borde do not get any recognition for successfully absorbing the most pressure, in Indian cricket history, of their teammates' wickets falling.

If the minimum criterion is fewer than 50 Tests, MAK Pataudi's contribution is especially significant as the man who absorbed the most pressure of falling wickets among all in the world, in 140 years of Test history. Sehwag, Azharuddin and Kapil Dev don't get their due for being the batsmen who most affected match results with their strike rate in Tests. Neither does Murali Vijay for having seen off the new ball more than any Indian opening batsman after Gavaskar, nor Azharuddin for being a bigger series-winner than Tendulkar in the 1990s, even if he had less impact overall.

• • •

How does context affect the Indian batting list? Let's start with the top five here. This is how they stack up, in order of their impact, with key batting parameters mentioned.

The big three are here, though not necessarily in the order you would expect. How does Kohli figure so high with an average less than 50? Why does the man with the highest average come in third? And how did someone with an average of 41.93 make the cut at all?

Dravid tops this list for two reasons. One, he is the biggest series-winner in Test history (alongside Inzamam-ul-Haq who also has eight series-defining performances, though in fewer matches) – a factor that must be taken into account when gauging the impact of any player. Two, his consistency marks him out, despite his poor run from 2007 to 2011.

Kohli, in the middle of his career, is enjoying a phase most players can only dream of (the series against Australia notwithstanding). His tendency to score big, once set, has taken him to these heights.

Viswanath makes this list because of his propensity to be a match- and series-winner, remarkable for a batsman as hopelessly attractive to watch, and for his ability to deliver often despite the carnage around him.

Laxman does not make this list because of his high failure rate – he did not bat

Batsman	Matches	Average	Bat Impact	SDs	RTI	Pressure Impact	Partnership Impact	Failure Rate (%)
Rahul Dravid	164	52.31	100	8	85	75	100	39
Virat Kohli	57	49.41	93	1	100	88	100	45
Sachin Tendulkar	200	53.78	92	6	84	72	77	42
Sunil Gavaskar	125	51.12	82	2	85	50	85	36
Gundappa Viswanath	91	41.93	80	3	74	100	69	43

NOTES

SDs = series-defining performances **RTI =** Run Tally Index

All impact parameters (apart from failure rate and SDs) are expressed on a scale of 0 to 100, with the maximum (100) assigned to the highest impact batsman from India in that parameter. All other batsmen are scaled relative to that

enough in positions most suited to him (Nos 3 and 4). That he could still be such a significant batsman in Indian Test history is a testimony to a once-in-a-generation talent. Sehwag does not get on either despite his status as a template-changing Test opening batsman. For all his dominating performances and big runs, he did not score nearly enough tough runs in his career. Curiously, it wasn't a problem with conditions as one would normally associate with a batsman as contemptuous of technique as him, but one of expectation: he seemed to play his best only if there was a clean slate or a licence to kill.

Now, to concentrate on the five who make the list. Let's begin with **Rahul Dravid** whose hallmark was big match play. As the table above also reveals, Dravid produced the most series-defining performances of any batsman in Indian Test history. He is also the best after Kohli when it comes to scoring the highest proportion of runs for his team and the most consistent batsman in Indian Test history after Gavaskar. But his most important characteristic was his ability to produce performances that decided series.

1996–2012 / 164 Tests / Average: 52.31 / 36 centuries / 63 fifties
Highest-impact performances:
270 v Pakistan, Rawalpindi, 2004
25 and 180 v Australia, Kolkata, 2001
81 and 68 v West Indies, Kingston, 2006

By our barometer, we study performances only in the context of a match – not merely an innings in isolation. It is not a coincidence that all of the performances listed above either decided or significantly shifted the momentum of a series. All three also resulted in historic wins. The fifties against West Indies, when Dravid batted for longer in both innings on a tough pitch than all the members of the opposition, is hardly remembered any longer. The performance most people would expect on this list – 233 and 72 not out in Adelaide in 2003 – is actually only his fifth-highest in terms of match-impact (fourth, if you consider series-impact). It is obviously not a coincidence that the timing of Dravid's best performances was even better than the finest on-drive he ever played: match-awareness – indeed series-awareness – like his is extremely rare, as Test history suggests.

Next on the list is **Virat Kohli** whose hallmark is his appetite for runs.

2011–present / 57 Tests / Average: 49.41 / 16 centuries / 14 fifties
Highest-impact performances:
167 and 81 v England, Vishakhapatnam, 2016
235 v England, Mumbai, 2016
115 and 141 v Australia, Adelaide, 2014

That he is the only one on this list who has scored more centuries than half-centuries – a rare and remarkable feat – reveals the bloody-mindedness with which he scores when set. He has 11 high-impact performances in 57 Tests, which is a pretty stunning rate. For perspective, Dravid has 22 in 164, Tendulkar 25 in 200, Gavaskar 15 in 125, Viswanath ten in 91, Sehwag ten in 103 and Laxman ten in 134. This is the main reason why Kohli has scored the highest proportion of runs in Indian cricket history to date (although Pujara, when he crosses 50 Tests, might trump him on this). This is also why he is so high impact, despite having just one series-defining performance to his name.

This propensity to score big runs has also made him the highest-impact No.4 batsman in Test history, for now, after Greg Chappell, Everton Weekes and Brian Lara. Apart from scoring the highest proportion of Test runs for India, he has also built the most partnerships (after Dravid) and absorbed the most pressure (after Viswanath and Borde).

Kohli's highest-impact Test performances were all on flat pitches – the first two in the same series, and the famous one at Adelaide in a losing cause. Despite big runs in all countries except England, it is too early to make a definitive call on whether Kohli can bat as well on difficult pitches and make tough runs.

Next on our list is **Sachin Tendulkar** whose hallmark was longevity.

Tendulkar's accomplishments are quite simply about volume. He holds the world record for the most runs and centuries and has a high average – the three most outdated means of judging batting talent. It's not that Tendulkar's natural talent or records can ever be in doubt, but the timing of his performances are another matter. Their metronomic regularity suggests that he played at the same level right through his career, without raising his game when the team needed it most (or not most of the time anyway, particularly in Tests). But he was there as an almost-omnipresent support act even in his series-defining performances – five of six such performances were as a support act. This explains his consistency rate

(third-best after Gavaskar and Dravid) and his high impact overall.

1989–2013 / 200 Tests / Average: 53.78 / 51 centuries / 68 fifties
Highest-impact performances:
5 and 55 v Australia, Mumbai, 2004
0 and 136 v Pakistan, Chennai, 1999
34 and 85 v West Indies, Mumbai, 1994

It is interesting how the list of highest-impact performances reveals so much about a player or his legacy. Two of Tendulkar's performances were in a support role (to Laxman and Manjrekar respectively) while the runs against Pakistan came in a losing cause. You'd be hard-pressed to find such a sequence in the best performances of any player, let alone one considered a legend. His most famous contribution in a winning cause (4 and 155 not out v Australia, Chennai, 1998) is his next highest-impact performance. However, given the context of the match, the performance that brought him the highest match tally of his career (241 and 60 not out, Sydney, 2004) is 47th on the impact list of Tendulkar's performances.

Fourth on this list is **Sunil Gavaskar** whose hallmark was consistency.

He is India's most consistent batsman and among the most consistent in the history of the game – remarkable for an opening batsman who undoubtedly faces the toughest challenge in the sport. He saw off the new ball better than any Indian batsman. He is also third in Indian cricket history with regard to building partnerships (after Dravid and Kohli) and scoring the highest proportion of runs for his team (after Kohli and Dravid). It must be remembered that the Indian team in his time were not world-beaters even though they had a few notable triumphs. They were often playing for draws where Gavaskar made the difference between defeat and a hard-fought draw.

1971–87 / 125 Tests / Average: 51.12 / 34 centuries / 45 fifties
Highest impact performances:
124 and 220 v West Indies, Port-of-Spain, 1971
21 and 96 v Pakistan, Bangalore, 1987
166 and 29 v Pakistan, Chennai, 1980

It's fascinating that Gavaskar's highest-impact performance came in his debut series (he produced a series-defining performance in his debut Test with 65 and 67 not out), and his next highest in his last Test innings. That classic innings of 96 – among the greatest final essays in cricket history – was tragic for another reason: India lost the Test by 16 runs in a fourth-innings chase and the series 0-1. If his team had scored another 17 runs, he would have had a series-defining performance. Similarly, his fourth highest-impact performance (13 and 221 v England, 1979) missed being a series-defining performance as India fell nine runs short of winning and could not level the series 1-1. These two missed opportunities in terms of series-defining performances would have doubled his count and brought him closer to Tendulkar's impact, which is remarkable given how much better the Indian teams were during Tendulkar's era. It also makes Gavaskar perhaps the unluckiest Indian Test player in terms of impact.

Finally, fifth on this list is India's man for a crisis – **GR Viswanath** whose hallmark was making tough runs.

Arguably the most stylish Indian batsman to play Test cricket, Viswanath was also the most reliable when it came to tough situations – there are few better examples of style and substance than this 5ft 3in package. A lot has been said about India not losing a single match in which he scored a century (14 in all), but no one has any other way of knowing that he absorbed the most pressure of falling wickets in Indian cricket history (minimum 50 Tests). He has also had three series-defining performances, one more than Gavaskar. This brings him close to Gavaskar's impact, which is remarkable given that they are separated by 10 runs in terms of averages.

1969–83 / 91 Tests / Average: 41.93 /14 centuries / 35 fifties
Highest impact performances:
52 and 139 v West Indies, Kolkata, 1975
97 not out and 46 v West Indies, Chennai, 1975
124 and 31 v West Indies, Chennai, 1979

Interestingly, each one is a crisis performance. The first two were from the same series (that India lost 2-3), and both the matches India won were on the back of Viswanath's performances even as wickets collapsed at the other end. The last one, against a Kerry Packer-hit West Indian side, came in a low-scoring match (he made 124 out of 255 and then 31 out of 125 for 7): India won by just three wickets in the end, the only positive result in six Tests. He also had a series-defining performance overseas – 114 and 30 v Australia, Melbourne 1981 – his next highest-impact performance.

• • •

It is essential to mention here that Cheteshwar Pujara will top this list once he crosses 50 Tests. He is India's highest-impact batsman, almost entirely based on what he has done for his team in subcontinental conditions. His batting average of 65 in 31 Tests is proof and his two series-defining performances even more so. His biggest quality is the high proportion of runs he has scored – fourth highest in Test history after Don Bradman, Jack Hobbs and Steve Smith – which would never stand out with his batting average just a touch above 50. A significant proportion were tough runs with Pujara having absorbed the most pressure by an Indian batsman at No.3.

While Pujara's batting average of 29.5 in 17 Tests outside Asia casts a dark shadow on his proposed greatness, it seems churlish to deny him that status in subcontinental conditions. He is the highest-impact batsman in 84 years of subcontinental Test history (all Tests in India, Pakistan, Sri Lanka, Bangladesh and even UAE considered) – ahead of legends like Dravid, Inzamam, Gavaskar, Laxman, Kohli, Tendulkar, Javed Miandad, Younis Khan, Kumar Sangakkara and Mahela Jayawardene. His role in India being the No.1 Test team is greater than anyone who holds a bat.

The best thing about Pujara's achievements is that he is a single-format batsman with not much of a role to play in limited-overs cricket. Even if you consider him a freak in today's Twenty20 world, it is clear that Test cricket is alive and kicking. The success of batsmen like Kohli, Murali Vijay and KL Rahul in both limited-overs and Test cricket proves that as well.

. . .

Photo: Clare Skinner

A WHOLE NEW BALL GAME

Liam Cromar reckons tennis could hold the key to cricket's future

It's played at Lord's. Its rules bewilder. It's been dubbed elitist and antiquated. And it most definitely is not cricket. Why? Because it's tennis.

By tennis, of course, we do not mean the glammed-up, boisterous, populist game played at Wimbledon, Flushing Meadows and Roland Garros. We are referring to the game of kings: real tennis, if one must use the vulgar.

An anachronistic oddity or a captivating spectacle? A sport disastrously out of touch with the public, or one proving faithful to its traditions? A game of alienating confusion or of enchanting subtlety? Wait, are we discussing real tennis or cricket? Both sports have a long and proud background, that much is understood; what is less recognised is how their stories intertwine, including the tennis connection to Lord's. Yet this shared history is no mere quirk, analogous to two people discovering their ancestors fought side by side in some ancient battle. In fact, real tennis's past may provide a glimpse into cricket's future.

A brief tour of real tennis at Lord's could start at the East Gate; bearing left, one passes the Mound and Tavern stands. Here, on the southern side of the ground, is where the first real-tennis court was built in 1839, by the entrepreneurial James Dark. According to Lord Aberdare's 1958 history *The Story of Tennis*, the court was demolished in 1898, but its surface was preserved and moved when the court was rebuilt on the southwest side of the ground. Cricket is not the only sport to feature an obsession with playing surfaces, it seems.

Walking on past the Grace Gates, we arrive at the MCC–Middlesex shop. The gentleman inside will gladly sell a famous pale-blue pamphlet – nearly as distinctive a colour in cricket as *Wisden* yellow. Inside, the 42 Laws of Cricket, source of such pleasurable confusion, stare impassively back. Laws, conduct, and governance: these are themes to return to.

Exiting the shop and continuing towards the Pavilion, we opt not to

go inside, and instead to escape the passing crowds (it is a match day) by diving through the doorway opposite, and arriving in the foyer of the MCC tennis courts. Left again, up a couple of steps, through a door and into the glass-backed viewing area of the dedans: we sit down, ready to be entertained by this most regal of games.

If a match is in progress, it will be difficult not to be drawn in by the court's asymmetry, the game's mystical rhythms, its beguiling patterns – aspects that cricket lovers are well placed to appreciate. While play is reminiscent of both squash and lawn tennis, the impression created by watching two highly skilled players – balls flying off every surface and angle, targets aimed for and missed – is of a sort of macro pinball.

Yet of more interest to us than either the game or the buildings is the role MCC has played in real tennis's development. It was more than 150 years ago, in 1866, that the St James court in Haymarket, at the time the sport's headquarters, closed its doors. The high-profile Varsity Match was relocated to the renovated court at Lord's, which became a natural point of focus for the administration of the game; thus, despite its name, MCC became tennis's governing body.

Like cricket, real tennis was set up to operate according to laws rather than rules. In 1872, MCC issued official Laws of [Real] Tennis. Even now, if you peruse the *Laws of Real Tennis* and the *Laws of Cricket*, you sense their shared ancestry. The injunctions of Law 15 sound particularly familiar: to "abide by the Laws and spirit of the game; [...]

not behave in any way likely to bring the game into disrepute".

As lawn tennis, in its different variations, arrived on the scene, MCC soon found themselves administering that too. MCC's Neil Robinson explains: "Lawn tennis in 1874 was in a similar situation to cricket in the early- to mid-1700s: the basic game was popular but played to a great variety of different local rules. From its experience with cricket, MCC knew that it was difficult to organise and develop a game without a unified code of Laws. [...] With real tennis long established at Lord's and the new game also popular, I think the Club felt ideally placed to provide guidance in this situation." Tennis historians David Best and Brian Rich confirm in their book *Disturb'd With Chaces* that MCC Secretary RA Fitzgerald suggested as much.

Fitzgerald, and MCC in general, had further justification for such a view, since they numbered George Lambert among their staff. He and his brother Charles, both tennis professionals, had a plausible claim to being the originators of the game. The Lambert family story was that, after a testy Marquess of Salisbury alleged tennis was unsuitable for ladies, the two brothers formulated an outdoor version.

Within a few years, George Lambert had moved to work at Lord's, and produced his own tennis sets, first sold to MCC members, then to the public. He also experimented on the Nursery Ground with various shapes and sizes of net and court. It was not long before the MCC Tennis Committee was in a position to consider the competing versions of the games, and issue the first official rules of lawn tennis. This it did in 1875, with the publication of the *"Laws of Lawn Tennis – Revised by the MCC"*.

Lawn tennis was on its way. Two years later, in 1877, the first Championships were held by the All England Club. In due course, the guardianship of lawn tennis passed on from MCC in 1883 and the AELTC in 1888, coming to rest under the remit of the newly formed Lawn Tennis Association. MCC continued oversight of real tennis, until its governance moved to the Tennis and Rackets Association in 1907.

The attitude of real-tennis players to the new upstart was not universally positive, even among those who took up the game. The winner of the second Lawn Tennis Championships, Frank Hadow, a rackets player and a first-class cricketer for Middlesex and MCC, declared it "a sissy's game played with a soft ball". Even the man he dethroned, Spencer Gore – the first Wimbledon champion, a real-tennis player and a Surrey cricketer – was unenthusiastic. Gore is reported as saying he thought lawn tennis was "rather boring and will never catch on".

It seems unlikely many would have predicted its sustained, explosive popularity. Leagues and associations sprang up all over the country, and it soon dwarfed its older relative. Tennis had been brought out into the light, quite literally, and it was blooming in the sun.

In the cloisters, real tennis continued to exist, but within a few decades was in serious trouble: the two World Wars, along with the Great Depression, had a devastating impact on participation. Its revival is a relatively recent phenomenon.

Cricket now faces its real-tennis moment. Limited-overs cricket has led to the Twenty20 revolution. Whereas one-day internationals were once regarded as short Test matches, in recent years the 50-over game has drawn closer in spirit to the 20-over format. The difference between the two fundamental forms of the game – red-ball or white-ball – has become more distinct.

In October, MCC will release the *2017 Code of Laws*. Their many deliberations have involved whether to include more reference to the limited-overs game, in recognition of its prevalence. Some would like to see the games formally split into two codes, claiming that a de facto split has already taken place, and that it is time to codify that gap. Simon Heffer, writing in the *Daily Telegraph*, maintained that it would be advisable to "plan the break, properly fund it, and give the traditional game a chance to survive". It would be easy, and wrong, to stereotype those who draw a line between the two forms as hidebound traditionalists: in an interview with Subash Jayaraman, published on ESPNcricinfo, Indian off-spinner Ravichandran Ashwin declared: "We can safely say that T20 cricket is another sport. It is probably not a part of cricket." Ashwin's comments are particularly noteworthy as he cannot be claimed as a Test loyalist nor a T20 revolutionary: at the time of writing, he is in the top ten of the ICC's rankings in both formats.

Could "real cricket" soon become a sport in its own right? It certainly is already in colloquial usage. It is almost unavoidable that, whenever T20 and first-class cricket are being discussed, sooner or later someone will claim the former is "not real cricket", or the latter is "proper cricket". Allied to this is the term "proper cricket shot", serving to imply that unorthodox shots – reverse sweeps, switch hits, scoops – are somehow improper.

Such concerns are nothing new. In the 1870s, a particular shot was described as an "offense to the spirit" and "spoiling the beauty" of the game. This was not cricket, however, but lawn tennis. The offending shot was the volley; despite being thus singled out for particular criticism in a manual by a Jasper Smythe, it formed a significant part of Gore's strategy in his 1877 Wimbledon win. Few would claim that volleying in the modern game does not enrich the sport.

Nor is the idea of something not being "real cricket" a recent development. In 1868, Anthony Trollope linked lack of public interest in a game between I Zingari and the Lords and Commons team to the fact that it was "thought not to be real cricket". There was some justification for that view: I Zingari fielded 11 players to the Lords and Commons' 22. The question is whether the view that T20 is bad for the game, corrupts our children, and is not "real", is similarly justified.

Take, for a moment, the inverse of "real" and "proper". "Unreal cricket"? An understandable description, perhaps, of the accelerated, manic game, with its otherworldly striking and levitational fielding, but hardly accurate: it belongs to the realm of reality rather than fantasy. "Improper cricket"? Cheerleading and the promotion of avarice may seem to be more closely associated with obviously crowd-pandering formats, but the rest of cricket can hardly claim to be exempt from such traits. "Fake cricket"? A term only justly levelled at fixed pseudo-contests. To borrow the rather self-laudatory County Championship 2016 hashtag: what do they know of #ProperCricket who only #ProperCricket know?

It is easy to decry anti-T20 opinions as archaic, and much too easy to dismiss them as the bacon-and-egg brigade's attempt to cling on to the past. Yet underneath the fear and loathing in the Warner Stand lies valid concern. As Ashwin, a highly successful exponent of both forms of the game, went on to point out, "the parameters that are addressed in [T20] are completely different to what is addressed in a one-dayer or a Test match". Although Ashwin here differentiates T20 cricket from one-day cricket, it follows that he considers the difference between T20 and Test cricket to be significant – potentially justifying classification as separate sports.

So is there, after all, a case for recognising "real" cricket as something distinct? Before that can be addressed, one has to get to grips with the almost deceptively simple question: what is cricket?

It is easier to start by considering what does not count as cricket. Presumably few followers of the game would have a problem with excluding Vigoro, the tennis–cricket hybrid from the early 1900s. But what about pairs cricket? Kwik cricket? Beach cricket? Somewhere along the continuum, the line has to be drawn; a sport ceases to become one thing and becomes another. This issue is raised most obviously when it comes to compiling statistics. *Wisden*'s Hugh Chevallier confirmed that, despite the lack of a hard-and-fast rule, it would be "highly unlikely" that the *Almanack* would "ever countenance" including such variants as six-a-side games, indoor cricket, and soft-ball games in the Records section; similarly, "gut feeling" would likely preclude achievements in an 11 v 22 contest, such as the I Zingari affair.

One option would be to take a strict definition of cricket as that which is played according to the Laws of Cricket. This sounds reasonable enough. The problem is that strictly adhering to such a definition not only disqualifies T20 with its Powerplays, fielding restrictions, and so on, but also Test cricket, relying as it does on a plethora of ICC-added regulations. A quick glance reveals that 25 of the 42 Laws are modified or overridden in some way for Test matches. First-class regulations allow replacing players. Tests prevent runners. Both are anathema to a purist, and yet form part of the purist's favourite form. Under such a definition of cricket, very few games today qualify as real, ironically even those one would automatically place in that category

Finding a game of cricket played only according to the Laws of Cricket and nothing else is the exception rather than the rule. So one could go to the other end of the spectrum, and declare cricket to be that which is based on the Laws of Cricket. The fact is, there is already flexibility in the Laws: numbers of players, length of innings, number of days are all accommodated. Limited-overs variants are also regulated, to

an extent, in the Laws. The advantage is that that is, more or less, the state of the game. The flaw is that, at least theoretically, one could override every Law and wind up with a game that is technically "cricket" without bearing any relation to the game as specified in the Laws.

Since it's hard to come up with a universally accepted definition of the game we love, it should be no surprise that the idea of "real" cricket is equally contentious. Some focus on the very real differences between the forms of the game, and claim they justify classification as different games; some insist that the no less real similarities prove the opposite. In fairness, however, it is reasonably easy to see what the defenders of #ProperCricket mean by the term: cricket that, firstly, is limited by time rather than overs, and secondly, preserves the four possible results – win, loss, draw and tie.

First-class cricket is the most obvious expression of this, and the County Championship probably trumps even Test cricket as the competition of choice, preserving that detached air of a game for the cognoscenti. Yet down at club level the same facets of the game can be witnessed, with draws (often oxymoronically described as "winning" or "losing" draws) a common feature in both friendly and league matches. Indeed, if you live in the UK, "real" declaration cricket is more likely to be found in your village than on your television.

Such popularity at what is termed "grassroots" level highlights one of the great differences between "real" cricket and real tennis. Real tennis never wished to conquer the world; on the contrary, in its very early days, it actively attempted to preserve its elite status by restricting the game to the nobility. By contrast, lawn tennis was unabashedly aiming for the mass market: both Spharistike and Germains lawn tennis, two of the proto-lawn tennis variants, were, after all, commercial products – the latter's official agents of distribution being, coincidentally, John Wisden & Co. When MCC and the All England Club revised its Laws in 1878, 1880 and 1882, the emphasis was on "recommending the game to all": a principle MCC continues to reflect in its guardianship of the *Laws of Cricket*.

As of 2017, there are around 6,000 players of real tennis in the UK. Now, 141 years after the codification of the Laws of lawn tennis, its progenitor continues to exist, with participation having increased steadily over the past 70 or so years; nevertheless, it is thoroughly eclipsed by its offspring. Real tennis, while conscious of the need to continue to acquire new players, has limited scope for doing so: it is hard to see how it could ever hope to acquire the same levels of worldwide popularity as lawn tennis.

The opposite is true – or should be true – of cricket. "Real" cricket is a game to be spread. There is a view that T20 is the game to spread the gospel of cricket unto all nations. While T20 may well be the most immediately effective method, it would be a mistake to limit such evangelism to that format: multi-day, first-class cricket, which provides its own beauty in an increasingly hectic world, is a blessing to be shared and spread.

Cricket would not benefit from a formal split between T20 and "real" cricket,

spinning T20 or limited-overs cricket off into a separate sport. Such a split could fossilise the "real" form of cricket. After all, the current popular view of real tennis, insofar as it penetrates public perception at all, is that of a strange oddity, a curiosity, almost a footnote – to the extent that while "tennis", strictly speaking, should mean real tennis, it almost always refers to lawn tennis.

In the 2017 version of the Laws, MCC, possibly cognisant of the history of their former ward, and wishing to avoid fostering disharmony and risking a full-blown schism, have opted against a wholesale split in codes – for the present. But, in time, cricket could benefit from formal definitions of the two main forms of the game.

In future iterations of the Laws, they could helpfully be reorganised into two categories: Laws common to both forms, and Laws that vary according to the form. The first category could include – all Law numbers as of the 2000 Code – Law 6 (The bat), Law 12 (Innings), Law 18 (Scoring runs), Law 21 (The result) and Laws 30–39 (various dismissals). Laws 12 and 21, however, which describing the victory conditions, would vary between the forms, as could a rewritten Law 41 (The fielder), which could codify additional fielding restrictions for limited-overs cricket.

Such an approach would emphasise the shared ancestry of both forms of the game, allowing them to grow and develop together, rather than in competition. It would help head off the danger of T20 developing in a way that ends up being divorced from its origins, a future where T20 defines its own equipment, laws, and definitions of fair play. Equally, it would help guard against first-class cricket retreating into its own cocoon, rejecting any modernising influence and gradually reducing its visibility: Tests, for example, would continue to enjoy the innovation introduced from limited-overs cricket, thus assisting in maintaining its spectator appeal.

Furthermore, the benefits would reach right into the recreational game. For real cricket, unlike real tennis, would be the simpler form. In real cricket, there would be no fielding restrictions and no bowling restrictions: two major reductions in complexity which lessen the load on captains and players.

There would be a need to select neutral terms to describe each variant. Real and Proper may be too loaded to use. Time cricket has the advantage of already being in casual usage, but sounds on the staid side. Clock cricket might

be an improvement, with the limited-overs version dubbed Countdown cricket – at the expense of sounding like daytime TV. Fixed and Flexi are other possibilities, despite carrying a hint of mortgage terms. Slow cricket could echo the "Slow TV" phenomenon, with its relative carrying the Speed moniker. As an alternative approach, in keeping with the cricket's infuriating penchant for homonyms (see "in", "out", "wicket", "pitch", etc), Line and Length cricket could provide endless confusion.

What's in a name, though? Whatever names they come to bear, both forms deserve to be nurtured; each can complement and contribute to the other. With proper care in development, in time we will be able to move beyond lazy dismissals of T20 as "not cricket", viewing both forms of cricket as siblings, worthy expressions of the great parent game of cricket – and both as real as the other.

. . .

THE HARROWING
OF THE NORTH

Winter skies over Durham. In the stratosphere
high winds stretch the clouds to thin scarves,
the moon in the bloom of a shawl, beneath
the long twilight, the heartbeat of the ground,
the shrouded wicket in hibernation, Kings bring
no gifts to lay on the turf on Twelfth Night,
the stable is empty of redemption, although
the evening star shines its solitaire diamond,
the ring of empty seats is not to be crowned.
The great cricket circle is that fairy ground
we do not trespass, sacred, holy, guarded
by the past, theatre of Albion's angels dressed
in white, a rite unconditional, fortress
of a treasure not to be bought or sold. Who
has entered the house and broken the hearth?
What vandal has clothed the air in despair?

The hearth goods ransacked. The empty seats
with no future. The Test lamp sentinels
with no switch. The embrace of the ground
is a widow without children. The vandals
entered without mercy. Struck down the pride
of Durham, put down the unarmed servants
in their quarters, the pennants were in tatters.
Sold off the warriors. Broke bonds of allegiance.
Men who are money Barons. They have no shame.
They are debt collectors. They scatter the village
and its green. They pillage what remains, the cups
looted from the cupboard. Mark them by their blows,
mark them by their words: This is a warning to others.
Eat grass. Eat the harshness of our deeds. Beg.
You are broken and defeated before the sun rises
and after the sun sets for five seasons by our reckoning,
shackled by our chains. Who will come to your aid?
We are dark lords. High winds racing above the earth
are turning clouds into scarves, the moon loses her shawl,
the ground is a shrine to the faithful, blessed by pilgrims.
Who will bring spear and sword? Jerusalem
was builded here among dark satanic mines.

S.J. Litherland

WHERE IS THE QUIET?

Tanya Aldred asks if there is any longer space for cricket as wallpaper

The United Services Ground, Portsmouth, 20 July 2000. Rahul Dravid is padding up for Kent and Shane Warne rolls out for Hampshire. The pitch is a belter and increasingly dry; the sky is dazzling cornflower. Around the rather utilitarian ground, people gather together on benches. The sun shines and the tinkle of the ice-cream van summons a constant trickle of overheated spectators to the pressurized nozzle of a 99. Barely anyone has a mobile phone, though lots of people carry a newspaper, and someone announces the scores from around the counties at lunchtime. Children play on the outfield. Warne pulls from his bag every trick and every ruse, once bouncing the ball high, way over Dravid's shoulder. But Dravid, a master of focus, leaves well alone and tarries away to a beautiful 137 before playing on to Hampshire's other leg spinner, Giles White. It is a day of cricketing perfection for those inside the ground, unfolding entirely at its own pace, independent of the outside world.

. . .

Cricket is frequently described as a passion. Engagement is either zippo or whoopee – a head-over-heels fervour from cradle to grave. The passage of time can be measured from a first excited scorecard-clutching trip, to walking in with a parent and having the pleasure of buying them a drink, to the passing of the torch on to children and then to grandchildren. It is a slightly faded but much-loved backdrop to a life trundling along.

But lately that cricketing wallpaper has become increasingly ATTENTION SEEKING. No longer content with just existing quietly, it pushes and pulls at us and demands our constant interactivity.

I will try not to serve up nostalgia-porn here, a cricket fan's most tempting dish. Cricket may never seem as good as it was when we were children, when batsmen wore caps, West Indies were unbeatable, the *Telegraph* printed the county averages and no one had thought up the abomination that is Cadbury's Dairy Milk Oreo Peanut Butter flavour. But it hurries along without us nevertheless.

It has to.

Life dictates that nothing discovered in the breathless flush of youth can ever be bettered by a bit of tinkering in middle age. But a moribund photograph of the cagouled 400 scattered about Grace Road damply turning the pages of the *Leicester Mercury* on a Thursday in May is not one the image-people like to see. And who can blame them? Whither vitality? Or joy?

Cricket in the UK has a big visibility problem. The stats that rocketed the ECB into its latest toying with the schedule were terrifying for a game that wants a future. Their survey showed that less than two per cent of children named cricket as their favourite sport. Only seven per cent put it in their top two. And when they were asked to name ten sports, three out of ten still didn't plump for cricket. The playing of the game falls off a cliff as adolescents enter their late teens. No child younger than 12 – in fact no one much younger than 17 – will remember watching cricket on terrestrial television. Unless you inherit a family devotion to the game, are lucky enough to play properly at school, or live near a club, you are unlikely to be remotely interested. Cricketers feature on adverts for Sky, but the chances of them appearing on television to extol the virtues of something like Shredded Wheat – as Ian Botham did in the 1980s – seem slim.

The game has had to fight for attention in a data-driven world, and has duly engaged. The England team and all the counties have social-media platforms. They will produce a meme of the day. A tweet of the day. Shot of the day. Stat of the day. Podcasts. Facebook chats. Players too engage direct with the public via social media. The race is on to get likes and retweets. Cricket on television encourages people to interact digitally, as does cricket on the radio. Cricket on the internet asks punters to not only keep an eye on over-by-over commentaries but also to join in below the line. A YouGov survey showed that 81 per cent of 13- to 18-year-olds own a smart phone – they love this stuff.

The noise is more than digital. On the pitch T20s, in particular, are a flamboyant, rowdy and loud experience. Shots are huge, music pumps out in frenzied bursts, spectators are encouraged to bang inflatable tubes together, and scream for the kiss cam. In this, cricket is only following the successful example of other sports – spectacularly, the 2012 Olympics and Paralympics. It brings life.

And yet. And yet. And yet.

In the haste to embrace the 21st century – for data, for noise, for interactivity – it seems we are starting to forget something fundamental: that watching and playing cricket has always had a meditative quality. The sheer size of the physical space in which the game takes place and the relatively slow-moving action plus interspersed periods of quietness – silence even – have always given spectators the freedom to be physically present while their spirit disengages. There is uninterrupted bliss in sitting quietly and reading a book, in talking to friends with cricket somehow easing the way to understanding and intimacy. For some, being able to watch every ball of a two-hour session whilst scoring with a stub pencil and balancing a tin-foiled square of peanut-butter sandwiches on a white fold-up seat is a special kind of heaven.

I wonder if the ECB haven't – in their headlong rush for the golden egg of T20 franchises – missed a trick. There was a need for more noise, to rescue a moribund game from turning in on itself, but the other quieter forms of cricket have a value too. For as much as we all chase our tails in a madcap attempt to keep up, we simultaneously want time out as well. Normal men and women – the type that might follow cricket – go on retreats. They seek out silence and sometimes solitude. Meditation and mindfulness apps are booming. Teenagers are encouraged to digitally detox. Individuals and firms, novelists and managing directors, pay to install social-media blocks on their computers.

The ECB have on their hands two products perfect for those seeking stillness. First, the County Championship, going since 1890 and still enjoyed in pretty much the same way as it was when parasols and thick scrubbing-brush moustaches were all the rage amongst the crowd. It offers a quiet, cheap, whole day's entertainment in a friendly community, where it is perfectly acceptable to sit and watch – or indeed not watch – alone. Here cricket can be a form of escapism for the stressed and the lonely, the bored and the broke, but also for anyone who would like to turn off and tune in to something completely different for a few hours.

How about promoting it as a stress-busting day out? A safe place to let children roam? GPs could be encouraged to recommend it to those suffering from anxiety or burn-out – an alternative to those mindfulness colouring books.

Punters could be promised from the outset: no pop music, no fireworks, no earpieces, and no forced interaction of any sort. Just remember to bring a coat.

The second meditative gem of the English game is recreational cricket. We went on Sunday to watch our daughter play, somewhere in a smart bit of Stockport, where dashing houses were chaperoned by mature trees. The ground was rectangular, with a small clubhouse nestled in the corner and wooden benches hunched hither and thither. At the neglected far fence, forget-me-nots competed with nettles for space, while bluebells spread themselves through the shade. An afternoon breeze ruffled the branches of the silver birch and every minute or so a chiff-chaff called. As a small slice of rural Eden, it was good enough.

Cricket has never existed in a noise vacuum. There has been bookmaking, betting, singing and rioting for as long as the game existed; the glory of the Port Elizabeth band, the banging rhythms of the Caribbean, the obsessive shouts for SA-CHIN have added colour and passion around the world. But what cricket has never done until the last ten years is demand so vociferously a person's undivided attention.

Just as the humble paperback has fought back against the seemingly inevitable march of the e-book, just as vinyl can still hold its own against the digital download, so modern cricket should be a little prouder and shout a little louder about the merits of its quieter side.

• • •

SNAP HAPPY

*The photographers who took the award-winning images for the
2016 Wisden–MCC Cricket Photograph of the Year, in association
with JP Morgan, tell us about how the images came about.*

SHORTLISTED Matthew Lewis (Getty Images)
West Indies captain Darren Sammy celebrates his team's victory over England in the final of the ICC World
Twenty20. Eden Gardens, Kolkata, India, April 3, 2016
*"The West Indies are always great to photograph as they show so much emotion. After all the
celebrations Darren Sammy lay on the ground and I think my picture shows the relief and ecstasy."*

SHORTLISTED Kuntal Roy (Amateur)

A young girl in a remote village is challenged by her friends to keep the ball bouncing on her bat. Sundarban, West Bengal, India. December 30, 2016

"This photograph was taken just 100 kilometres away from my home town Kolkata. Where I travelled into the village I saw some boys preparing for cricket and few Muslim girls looking over and just relaxing beside the playground in their burkhas. I love them playing cricket with their traditional veiling."

SHORTLISTED Md Rafayat Haque Khan (Amateur)

On a winter morning in the Brahmanbaria District of central Bangladesh, children play cricket among drying rice. Chittagong, Bangladesh November 3, 2016

"I was staying in the rice mill area of B. Baria, Bangladesh to get the story of rice mill workers when I suddenly saw these children playing cricket in the rice mill yard."

SHORTLISTED A. M. Ahad (Freelance)

Children play cricket on a road in Sirajganj, Bangladesh. February 4, 2016

"The village is about 60 miles north west of Dhaka, Bangladesh. I used a 35mm focal tenth shot to give the sense of the place. I watched their game for a long time. It's interesting that children prefer cricket in every corner of the country where they used to play soccer, especially in villages."

SHORTLISTED Matthew Childs (Action Images)

Jos Buttler and Joe Root dive for a catch in the Fifth England v Sri Lanka One-Day International. SSE SWALEC, Cardiff, Wales. July 2, 2016.
"It was the final game of the one day series. I was happy with the pictures I had got throughout the series but had little or nothing on the wicket-keeper. I had spent the morning session in a head-on position while England were batting but moved for the afternoon session to try and get some variation in what I was doing. I set aside a few overs to concentrate on the wicket-keeper and within the first over I got the frame of Jos Buttler and Joe Root diving for the ball in opposite directions. I couldn't believe how fortunate I was."

SHORTLISTED Ash Allen (Ash Allen Photography)

Lendl Simmons of St Kitts and Nevis Patriots loses his bat during a game against Trinbago Knight Riders in the Caribbean Premier League. Central Broward Regional Park, Fort Lauderdale, Florida, USA, July 31, 2016
"This match was my first trip covering cricket in America. And what a venue! The stadium had an electrifying atmosphere and there was a great mix of travelling fans from various Caribbean Islands and locals, all cheering wildly for their respective teams. In this image, Lendl Simmons was going all-out to heave a six over midwicket when he lost control of his bat."

SHORTLISTED Paul Miller (Australia Associated Press)

Pat Cummins of Sydney Thunder fails to hold a catch offered by Moises Henriques of Sydney Sixers during a BBL Twenty20 match. Spotless Stadium, Sydney, Australia. December 20, 2016

"Twenty20 cricket moves so quickly that it is easy to miss things when you're trying to shoot and file with a lot happening in a short period of time. It makes it that bit harder when you miss seven overs getting to the other side of the field and back chasing what you hope will be an epic sunset! This is the gamble I took, and it did not pay off as the sunset didn't eventuate and I missed quite a few wickets as I was spending the whole time looking through a wide angle lens. I reluctantly filed my 'sunset' pictures and readied myself for the second innings. But on the upside I did manage to get this shot!"

RUNNER-UP

Asanka Brendon Ratnayake (Freelance)

Virat Kohli warms his hands during the second Australia v India T20 International. Melbourne Cricket Ground, Australia, January 29, 2016

"Whether it's a President, dignitary or in this case a sports superstar, I always try really hard to get photos of them with their guard down. It was a pretty cold day at the MCG, the match was a pointless T20 international and no one took it seriously. Virat is a serious guy, it's hard to get him with his guard down, and in this instance I got my 'off' moment without trying. Moral of the story, 'don't try so hard' or maybe I should just photograph more meaningless T20 internationals?"

RUNNER-UP

Philip Brown (Freelance)

Shakib Al Hasan bats on the second day of the First Test between Bangladesh and England Zohur Ahmed Chowdhury Stadium, Chittagong, Bangladesh October 21, 2016

"I found one spot in the ground that had a lovely dark background late in the afternoon. I spent about an hour working with that background and on the second afternoon Shakib Al-Hasan was attacking the bowling and lots of dust was being disturbed. I was scrabbling around on my knees moving about after nearly every ball to get in the perfect position. The light reflecting off the bat was a real bonus but I can say I don't think I've ever worked as hard to get a photograph. I think I deserved a little slice of luck."

**WINNER Saqib Majeed
(Freelance)**

Kashmiri Muslim boys play
cricket under autumn shades in
the Nishat Bagh gardens on the
outskirts of Srinagar Indian-
administered Kashmir November
10, 2016

*"Engineer by profession and
photographer by passion.
Nature has been always a
blessing to me and Kashmir
is known for it. Landscape
photography has remained
my basic attraction. It has
been my desire to introduce
the beauty of my motherland
– Kashmir – to the world.
Autumn has always been
nearest to my heart. It
somehow reflects Kashmir –
colour, pain, agony, fire, smoke
and beauty. After covering
the bloody summer agitation
in Indian-controlled Kashmir,
my heart and mind were
searching for something to
soothe aggravated minds. I
went to Nishat Garden, one of
the famous Mughal Gardens of
the Kashmir. As I was walking,
I saw a group of boys playing
cricket under the chinar trees,
Woah! I remember that scene.
It was like white tulips tossing
heads in the fire pool. I took
up a best possible position,
some 35 feet above the field
where the boys were playing.
To me the image has a lot of
stories, it isn't just a glorified
picture of cricket or the
colours of autumn. It is a sign
of the 'life' when everything is
smuggling death."*

STROLL ON

Peter Hanlon celebrates a Fleet Street institution

Brian Taylor recently turned 70, stands tall at the crease and cover drives with an elegance bettered only in his imaginings. His old Nottingham High School friend Simon Brodbeck reached the same lofty score a couple of months earlier, finished last season with two wickets and a run-out in a tight win, and remains as hard to shift at the crease as he is a genteel presence either side of the boundary. Peter Patston is 67, indomitable, but concerned that Parkinson's disease is sapping the fizz from his off-breaks. They've known each other for 40 years, because they were then and are still teammates. Moreover they are Fleet Street Strollers, and when this is your boast, why ever would you consider stopping?

We don't have cricket clubs like the Strollers in Australia, more's the pity. It's easy to pass this off as a function of cliché – to conclude that in a boisterous, hairy-chested sporting landscape the sole motivation for playing at any level is to win, and all other considerations are pushed to the margins. It's easy to imagine that in such an environment,

cricketers at the bottom of the pyramid are bound to similar use-by dates as those at the top.

I'm not entirely sure that summation fits. Cricketers down under play for the love of the game too, for camaraderie, and in the hope of slowing time's irrepressible hands. But the structure – of clearly defined competitions underpinned by points, ladders and the quest to find the best – unashamedly promotes attrition. It's the only way most Australian cricketers know. Perhaps that would be different if more had experienced the enchantment of the Strollers.

I returned to the rural Victoria of my upbringing a few years ago and found that the cricketers of my youth were either wallowing in middle age or had become lawn bowlers, a pursuit that feeds their competitive juices without demanding reflexive avoidance of a fast-moving missile, and leaves a much shorter walk to the bar. I opted instead for a return to competitive cricket. At 48 I'm a source of amusement and a subject of derision to everyone. Thankfully I

have a bald, 52-year-old spin-bowling teammate who, despite finishing the 2016–17 season as our leading wicket-taker, is still generally regarded as a geriatric freak who should know better. As your shadow lengthens, it's nice to have someone to hide behind.

The previous Australian summer, Brian and Tricia Taylor visited from the UK and stayed with us at the height of the cricket season. Brian had packed his whites, his batting gloves and his box, a hat-trick of hints that led to a couple of net sessions in which my Birregurra CC teammates were initially greatly amused ("Pete, you're fucking kidding, aren't ya?"), and soon just as greatly impressed ("Shit, the old bloke can still play!"). On two Saturday afternoons, play Brian did – without mishap or disgrace. He's quietly chuffed to now boast of being the oldest debutant in Colac District Cricket Association history, and a little miffed that he wasn't batted higher up the order.

I know that in the broad church of English cricket there have always been teams with elements of the Fleet Street Strollers, conjured up and cobbled together to satisfy a simple yearning to play the game. Their members aren't exclusively ancient, nor are they hopeless; like the Strollers, the age range spans many decades, and abilities are dotted along a similar spectrum. Many of these sides peter out after a generation or so, unable to find new custodians prepared to take middle and leg in an increasingly busy world. The Strollers, meanwhile, just keep getting stronger.

Over lunch on a drizzly January Isle of Wight afternoon, Simon, Peter and Brian filled in the blanks. The club started in 1976 as a newspaper office team thrown together when John Marshall, a former editor of the now defunct *Evening News*, was scouting for opposition for his West Chiltington village team. "We were heavily outclassed," Simon recalls. The seeds of a credo – "We may be embarrassed next week" – were sown.

Peter Patston had played what he calls "some Fleet Street cricket" with a *Sunday Express* team, where luminaries such as Ted Dexter and Denis Compton would "turn up, stroll around, score a hundred, take five wickets then breeze off." Simon and Peter met playing an annual game between the *Evening Standard* and the *News*. In early Strollers matches they'd toil away unchanged from either end, 16 or 17 overs at a time, largely because nobody else could string even a couple together. Brian Taylor recalls Peter bowling medium pace sporting a perm. Simon remembers a bubble cut.

Beginnings were humble. "The height of our ambition was not to lose," Simon says. "We became very good at draws." They even had "specialist draws players", like veteran Fleet Street hack John Smyth who could routinely bat for two hours, barely reach double figures, but keep the enemy at bay.

At length the late Reg Cooper – an *Evening News* features desk stalwart and enthusiast in sport and life (who Simon graciously calls "our founding father") – drove the adoption of a name and the expansion of the fixture list. With more games came new challenges. "You'd wander down Fleet Street and go into a pub on Tuesday night – the Cheshire Cheese, the Harrow, the Old Bell," Peter says. "And you'd have 11 fit men, perhaps 12 or 13. Come Sunday morning they'd have all disappeared. Of course there were no mobile phones or email to chase them down, so you had to be inventive."

Simon takes up the story: "Legend has it there was a number in Earl's Court you could ring and ask for a cricketer. The phone would be answered by an Australian voice: 'Yeah mate, oi can play. And oi can bring a cupla mates, too.' You'd arrive at the ground on Sunday and they'd be there." So began another Strollers' tradition – the embrace of anyone, from anywhere, as long as you played the game the right way.

I came to the Strollers in the usual manner – via journalism. Three months into a planned two-year stay I was running out of money, desperately in need of work, and peering glumly at London in mid-winter from inside a rain-streaked public phone box. I fished out a number provided by a Melbourne journo colleague, found a 10p piece, and rang the *Daily Express* sports desk.

"Do you play cricket?" asked the Lord of the Rota, Simon Brodbeck.

"Um, yes."

"Bat or bowl?"

"Bat."

"Right, you'll get three shifts a week if you can play every Sunday. If you start taking Sunday shifts somewhere else, you'll be out."

Many years later, writing a piece for a coffee-table book that explored the essence of Australian cricket, I interviewed Alan Turner, who opened the batting under a baggy green cap in 14 Tests in the 1970s. He told of playing Sunday games for the London Cricketers Club while on the 1975 Ashes tour in the hope of finding form ahead of the inaugural World Cup. "You'd get fifty, get out, sit down and they'd give you a beer," Turner said. Fielding on the fence in the milky late-afternoon sunshine, he was served port out of the back of a Bentley. "I thought, 'This is living, this is great.'"

On picture-postcard village greens – against Windsor and Henley, Hurley and Great and Little Warley, and in the middle of Royal Ascot racecourse where above the pavilion door hung a team photo with the Queen Mum front and centre – the Strollers have given me that joy. It wasn't all about setting and socialisation, although the fulfilment of making runs on the sloping ground that Laurie Lee gifted the Cotswolds village of Sheepscombe is equalled by the memory of two teammates limbering up that day with a bottle of red wine and a joint.

A love of touring has always been an essential part of a Strollers' make-up. A 1977 excursion to the Forest of Dean pre-empted the still-going-strong Cotswolds and Three Counties tours. Annual treks to Brittany and the Riviera have rounded out a delectable "extras" column on the calendar. Bringing wives, partners and friends (bat or bowl?) is actively encouraged. Simon, more temperate than many fellow tourists, is happy to retire to bed when post-dinner conviviality rises. "They can do whatever they like, as long as they appear on the field."

Others are harder to shift. One long night in Ashby de-la-Zouch, Peter's usual practice of taking new Strollers tourists under his wing led to a 5am "net" on a neighbouring pitch, a pint mug for the wicket with a shoe placed on a length. "We were discussing leg-break bowling, one thing led to another," Peter says. "We couldn't hit that bloody shoe at all."

Having Fleet Street in the name helps in attracting both new players and opposition. A handful of journalists remain on the books, and although the club crest (three quills as stumps with the middle one being bowled over) and colours (black and white and red all over) are a nod to a lost and lamented newspaper age, no professional or personal elitism is tolerated. Only the overly fervent who refuse to bend to the Strollers way – "competitive, but in a friendly fashion" – are shunned. "We're deliberately not playing league cricket," Simon says.

The numbers are impressive – more than 1,100 games played, north of 700 cricketers around the world proud to say they've been a Stroller, even if hundreds of them did so only once. "You look through the list and say, 'Who's he? I can't remember him,'" Simon says. "Which is a bit sad."

The saturation of statistics on the club website is down to Peter's wife, Maggie, who having read maths at university in 1977 unwittingly found herself the ideal candidate to become official scorer. During last season, the Strollers' 40th, Maggie scored her 600th game. Original records are stored at home in Bath – "in the bunker at Patston Towers, in case of enemy attack," says Simon – and have been painstakingly digitised in recent years. It's been a labour of love, one well understood by their three daughters. Maggie recalls breastfeeding being timed around tea intervals, babies being settled and walked by Strollers (presumably in a stroller), Amanda being taught to count by one wag who thought it would be funny to skip the numbers from 11 to 19. "Of course, Amanda believed him rather than her parents." Peter says their family was brought up on the boundary line. Maggie reflects that no harm was done. "They thrived, we survived and the club went strolling on."

The stats detail dark days (all out for eight v Blackfordby, 27 August 1988), and stunning individual efforts, many in recent times by a committed cohort of New Zealanders. One, Jono Addis, made double-hundreds two years running against the same opposition – in 40-over games. Another, James Timperley, has notched up 18 hundreds and more than 50 half-centuries in just nine brilliant seasons. They've had some seriously good players.

And some wonderful servants. Simon Brodbeck has played more than 700 games, taken close to 1,100 wickets, made almost 8,000 runs. His ambitions now are a modest delight. "I quite like the shape of the day. Even if I don't do anything particularly in a match, just seeing the day's events unfold, the game swinging that way and this way, and seeing other people do well."

Peter Patston (600-plus appearances, 4,000 runs and 700 wickets) is spurred by the condition that changed his world early in 2015. In March he ran the Bath half-marathon. He still believes wholeheartedly that he's worth his place in a decent Strollers side. "Parkinson's is a bit of a headache, but I want to keep living as normally as possible and cricket's part of that. Besides, I still think I can get better, I really do."

Brian still plays for his club side, Stanton By Dale, and his quest for cricketing nirvana continues. One afternoon last season, he almost found it. "Nice ground, lovely batting wicket – nice and hard, coming on to the bat. Stepped out to an off-break bowler and stroked the ball back past him." In the seconds that followed – watching something you've propelled through a sweet confluence of hand and eye and

body moving in time, run away across a green field and over the boundary – a cricketer is ageless. For a moment, life's grains stop slipping through the fingers. And the heart sings with a joyous affirmation: I can still do it!

Next February, the Strollers are planning to stretch their legs and reconnect with their Kiwi brethren on a New Zealand tour. My club, Birregurra, is about to turn 150. Moves are afoot to lure the tourists into an Australian stopover on their way home. It's time for a game and a celebration of cricket and life. If it's agreeable, I'd like to swap sides and make my 26th appearance for the Strollers spanning almost 25 years. I reckon we could teach the locals a thing or two about how cricket should be played.

. . .

AM I LOOKING AT YOU?

Paul Edwards on cricket photographs

"The beauty of it is that I can't imagine the images I'm going to send out that day." – photographer Philip Brown

My school had a fine library and I made good use of it. Before long the librarian trusted me to visit the dusty stacks where old *Wisdens* were shelved in bookcases that faced each other with less than a boy's width between them. Hour after hour I wedged myself into a small chair and read about cricket matches in Dover, Glastonbury, Eastbourne. Himalayan peaks could not have exerted a more powerful grip on my imagination. But it was not the closely-printed Almanacks which most held my attention; that bizarre honour fell to a folio volume ornately decorated in dark green cloth with its title printed in faded gold letters: *The Book of Cricket: A New Gallery of Famous Players*. Although the tome was edited by CB Fry and included his pen-portraits of the players, the majority of the pages were dominated by photographs. In those days I knew only some of the cricketers posing for the camera but I had the curious sensation that these people's lives were, in some

way yet to be defined, my business. "Account for us," they seemed to be saying, "Tell our stories."

The Book of Cricket is an odd mixture. Published in 1899, a mere 42 years after the oldest surviving photograph of a cricket match was taken, it presented its readers with the leading players of the day in a variety of poses or action shots. There are also team pictures and ground views. *The Daily Mail* saluted Fry's book as "the most remarkable record of cricket ever put between two covers," an accolade which was probably justified when one considers the book's early attempt to capture action with equipment barely fit for the purpose. The most impressive photographs are those which achieve that ambitious goal. As Fry himself completes a shot towards midwicket the ball speeds through the air towards the camera at short mid-on. Underneath is the jocular caption: "Aimed at the Artist." There is so much that appeals to me about William Rouch's photograph, not least its apparent spontaneity and the Victorian villas standing behind the high

wall of the unnamed cricket ground. But to describe a photographer as "an artist" may have seemed particularly daring in 1899. Aesthetes might query what exactly a person with the camera did but take a picture of what anyone else could see in the first place? Only 40 years previously the French poet Charles Baudelaire had come in off his full run: "If photography is allowed to stand in for art in some of its functions it will soon supplant or corrupt it completely, thanks to the natural support it will soon find in the stupidity of the multitude."

Fry's book seems to me to be the record of a medium attempting to understand its potential. One of the most impressive brief sequences shows the Warwickshire medium-pacer Sydney Santall at three points of his run-up and delivery stride. One is able to visualise Santall's action and the effort that went into it. In contrast to the action shots were the unconsciously amusing posed portraits: the plump Hampshire off-spinner Harry Baldwin, doing nothing more threatening than pulling his flannels up beyond his waist, above the caption, "The Cheery Bowler"; Bernard Bosanquet grimly clutching a two-handed caught and bowled in a pastoral setting – some of the pitches in the book look more like rough lawns – above the command. "You Must Go."

Team photographs were no less fascinating. One shows ten of the Gentlemen who defeated the Players by an innings and 59 runs at Lord's in 1899. (Kent's Jack Mason is absent and I have frequently wondered why.) All the cricketers are wearing blazers and a couple are sporting boaters. One can only imagine the kaleidoscope presented to Rouch's eye and, perhaps,

his frustration that this riot of colour could not be captured by his camera. The professional umpires, Mordecai Sherwin and Bill West, are standing on the back row of the picture, their presence tolerated by the victorious amateurs even if their initials are omitted from the names below the photograph.

Such a distinction is even clearer in my framed photo-print, taken by Waterlow and Sons, of the England side that defeated Australia by an innings and 137 runs at The Oval in 1888. This victory brought the series level at 1-1 and the discrimination some thought necessary is rigorously maintained in the composition of the picture. The three amateurs, WG Grace, John Shuter and Walter Read are given seats on the middle row; they had also taken three of the first four places in the batting order. The only professional allowed a chair is Billy Barnes, who took seven wickets in the match. The photograph invites speculation and research. In how many environments apart from this one and the field of play might the trio of amateurs have been seen with the professionals? Are George Lohmann and Frank Sugg deliberately trying to look casual by standing with their hands in their pockets on the back row? Can we detect challenges to authority in the expressions on the faces of Bobby Abel and Johnny Briggs, both of whom are sitting cross-legged on the grass? You would need to see the photograph to answer the latter question but the richness of the medium seems plain. Whatever these players might be revealing, the differences between their attitudes and the quietly smiling, uniform confidence of 21st-century Team England are striking.

For all its many merits *The Book of Cricket* hardly suggests that six years later George Beldam would take what is still often regarded as the greatest cricket photograph of all. True, the skills of Beldam, Rouch et al were gaining respect. In 1901 they had received the acclamation of George Bernard Shaw: "If you cannot see at a glance that the old game is up," he wrote, "that the camera has hopelessly beaten the pencil and paintbrush as an instrument of artistic impression, then you will never make a true critic: you are only, like most critics, a picture fancier." Yet Beldam and Fry knew that something more was needed if action photography was to convince the Baudelaires of its worth. In two books they aimed to provide it. The first was *Great Batsmen: Their Methods at a Glance* and it included *that* photograph of Victor Trumper "Jumping Out for a Straight Drive," which was almost certainly taken in May 1905 and has since bewitched most of those who have seen it. In their introduction to this book, Fry and Beldam offer a declaration of purpose, one which all subsequent cricket photographers would probably sign:

"It has been said that the results of instantaneous photography, however true to nature, are generally inartistic in effect: 'very true but very ugly.' Possibly such an opinion may be revised in the light of a study of these pictures of live cricket. Some of the attitudes may seem strange and unfamiliar to those who have never studied great batsmen in action with very close attention. But some of them go to prove how beautiful a game is cricket, and to suggest that the sculptor of modern times might possibly achieve statues of athletic perfection in nowise inferior to those of ancient Greece in the age of the athletic prizemen.

"Apart from the purely technical aspect of the art of batsmanship in these pages, we hope that the pictures have caught something at any rate of the glow and glory of 'the game with the beautiful name.'"

Suddenly the bar had been set at a height few could reach. The sense of movement, the intensity of intention and the definition of the musculature in Beldam's photograph have lost none of their power. The potency of the image is analysed superbly in Gideon Haigh's book, *Stroke of Genius*, which included this comment from 2008 by the Australian prime minister Kevin Rudd: "You *know* that photograph. It just sits in your mind and your memory."

Lord's, 5 April 2017. I am attending the *Wisden* dinner and it is perhaps my favourite evening of the year. All the fragile, bright incipience of an English cricket season is concentrated into a few hours. I enjoy the occasion so much that I arrive as early as possible and stroll around, trying to avoid the necessary attention of closed-circuit TV and amenable stewards. On the big screens at each end of the almost deserted ground are shown the shortlisted contenders for the Wisden–MCC Cricket Photograph of the Year. Here, too, there is something of Fry and Beldam's "glow and glory" of cricket, not least in Saqib Majeed's winning picture of an autumnal game in Srinagar, Kashmir. Taken from high vantage somewhere on the point boundary, it shows a seemingly informal match taking place on a brown field with the overhanging trees wearing a confection of red and gold leaves. The cricket is framed by its environment, rather as Fry had been when he posed for Rouch nearly 120 years earlier.

Cricket and its photography have changed so much since *The Book of Cricket* was published; yet they have also barely altered at all. Beldam cleared a path which others have turned into a broad highway. Improvements in equipment, greater access to the players and an increasingly sophisticated awareness of the medium's capability produced a far wider range of photographs on all subjects in succeeding decades of the 20th century. The consequences were crisply assessed by the American journalist and political commentator Walter Lippmann in 1922: "Photographs have the kind of authority over imagination today, which the printed word had yesterday, and the spoken word before that."

Some years before Lippmann made his observations an unnamed Press Association photographer had taken a head-on shot of a young Jack Hobbs jumping out to drive, his bat poised at the top of the backswing and the front foot airborne. The echoes of Beldam's Trumper are unmistakable and unsurprising. This was another photograph which transcended its artificial context. "It is possible to believe in this picture," suggests Nick Yapp in *Caught in the Frame: 150 Years of Cricket Photography*, "This is not a man posing for the camera, but the greatest batsman in the world revealing a little of his brilliance." A similar judgement may be made about the famous picture taken by Herbert Fishwick of the *Sydney Mail* when he captured Walter Hammond completing

one of his signature cover drives during his innings of 225 in the MCC v New South Wales game in November 1928. And it was the photographer's art as well as the batsman's majesty which inspired Alan Ross to write "A Photograph of Hammond", one of his nine cricket poems: "Even at 1/500th you can't freeze him, / Make his image quite static. / He remains more mobile than diagrammatic. [...] Never mind the earthbound heaviness / Of hip, of shoulders, his cover-drive / Evokes airiness, an effortless take-off." What I like about all this is the interplay of forms, the way in which Fishwick helped Ross, quite late in his life, to see something new in a batsman he will almost certainly have watched in the flesh. The photographer prompted the poet to look again.

Fishwick, of course, was using film and had to develop his photographs. The need to employ such techniques seems quaint in the 21st century and, when the next history of photography is written, the move to digital technology will be seen as the greatest revolution in the development of the medium. Indeed, it has led some of cricket photography's most eminent and skilled practitioners to reassess the state of their art.

"The first time I was sent to a Test match was 1988 and I could possibly take three frames a second," says Philip Brown, a leading sports photographer for over 20 years. "With digital cameras I can take 12 frames a second and there is auto-focus, so as long as you point the camera at the target area and it picks up something to focus on, you should be alright. When I started you had to turn the barrel of the lens so – and I know this sounds like an old bloke complaining – there was a real skill involved in when to take the photo and getting it in focus. You have to take your hat off to people like Patrick Eagar, Adrian Murrell and Ken Kelly.

"You don't have to worry now about taking the photo at the right moment and it's not a financial decision as to when to take a photo. In the 1990s I couldn't go back with 18 rolls of film and say 'I've done the cricket today.' You had to go back with four rolls, so you were limited to 140 pictures or you looked like an idiot. You had to think whether something was worth taking. It might cost 40p every time you took a photo; now, if you have a flash card or memory card in your camera, you can fill it up with 10,000 photos and press another button to wipe it.

"Photography had stayed the same with film and developing and so on for over 100 years. I was at The Open golf when digital was demonstrated and I didn't realise how much things were going to change. Eventually even the traditional photographers had to change. The timing is different, though. The amount of skill you need is limited now and it used to be a real competition."

Yet a few minutes before voicing those misgivings, Brown had been reflecting with justified pride on a moment when his skill and experience had been most obviously in evidence. On the third afternoon of England's one-sided Test against India at Old Trafford in 2014 Stuart Broad hit Varun Aaron for successive sixes. Brown describes what happened next:

"I was thinking that I needed to be ready because he was on the attack. And the next ball went straight through his grille and into his nose. In my first frame the ball was seven feet from his face; in the second it was on his nose. You have to have that element of luck. I think Stuart later said to me, 'Great shot.' There's still a thing about having an eye for the picture that works."

Brown's splendid picture appeared in the 2015 *Wisden*; indeed, the Almanack frequently features his work and did so again in 2017 when his shot of Shakib Al Hasan's shining bat was one of the runners-up for the photograph of the year award. However, the picture I liked most in this year's *Wisden* featured that by-now-famous game when Ben Stokes and the rest of Durham's players stayed in Southport after they had beaten Lancashire and played cricket on the outfield with a couple of the club's juniors. I was alone in the press tent that evening and have since written about it. But none of my words come close to capturing the moment as well as the Durham captain Paul Collingwood's pictures of Stokes batting against Peter and Tom Crew on a golden evening. But that is what images can do: they take us from Srinagar to Southport. Perhaps I had an inkling of it in my school library all those years ago; certainly it now helps me understand the work of Philip Brown and his green-bibbed colleagues on the morning of a Test match when they venture out to the boundary edge, release their shutters and capture the beauty of the unimagined instant.

Paul Edwards would like to thank Philip Brown very much for taking time out to discuss cricket photography with him.

• • •

THE BOY WHO BOWLED HUTTON

Patrick Ferriday talks to a man who made a startling debut

Robin Thorne was still a few months shy of his 19th birthday when he made his debut for Border at the Jan Smuts ground in East London. The opposition was the 1948–49 MCC touring side, leading a five-match series 1-0 after three games and halfway through an arduous 22-match tour. When Thorne took the new ball just before the close on day one, Border had struggled to 156 off the MCC front-line attack minus a resting Alec Bedser. The opening batsmen were Len Hutton and Cyril Washbrook, who had taken 359 off South Africa in the second Test before being parted. The task facing the teenager could fairly be described as daunting.

The inevitably nervous Thorne was dispatched for two fours in his first eight-ball over but in his second, Hutton, with just five to his name, was left groping at a good-length ball that pitched outside off and came back through the gate before hitting off stump. For the next ten years and more Thorne would be known as "the boy who bowled Hutton". This epithet's most recent application was fully 62 years after the event.

With typical modesty Thorne's reflection is that it was a fluke – his usual method was outswing at military medium pace and this ball "must have caught the seam". Thorne's teammates and parents were delighted but the crowd less so; the majority had come to see the great Hutton bat and not some unknown teenager bowl. A visiting Yorkshireman and county teammate of Hutton's, Harry Halliday, saw an opportunity for some humour at the expense of the master batsman. He offered to take Thorne and a precious copy of the photographic evidence into the England dressing room to seek Hutton's signature. The great Len was less than amused and signed the offending paper with no eye contact while Halliday vigorously chewed his hand to restrain gales of laughter that were threatening to flood out.

Sixteen years later Thorne made his final first-class appearance on the same ground against the same opponents. This time the openers were Geoff Boycott and Mike Brearley. Once again MCC were leading the series 1-0 with two to play and were in the process of thrashing Border, needing just 53 to win in their second innings. Only one wicket fell and again it was a future England captain, bowled Thorne for five, although this time it was not a Yorkshireman.

These are the bookends to a career limited by work and the structure of South African cricket. Now living in a picturesque cottage in Berkshire, the robust and witty Thorne with his wife Mary – a long-time scorer at club and provincial level – by his side, can detail what lies between the bookends. With astonishing recall, verve and wonder he recounts how lucky he was to play with and against legendary players like Bruce Mitchell, Neil Harvey, Ted Dexter, the Pollock brothers, Brian Statham and Alan Davidson.

Thorne was born in Port Elizabeth in 1930. His grandfather had emigrated from Britain to the Orange Free State in 1870 in search of fresh, dry South African air for his consumptive lungs. His father fought in German South West Africa and German East Africa in the First World War. Thorne spent the Second World War years in Cape Town, and vividly recalls the sight of 70 allied warships in the harbour, having dodged a strong U-boat presence and preparing to do so again. But there were no bombardments, air raids or rationing so life was more American than British despite the activities of numerous German spies, a source of pride to Lord Haw-Haw back in Berlin.

By this time the sports bug had bitten but there was precious little coaching of any sort to be had at school in Cape Town or at his new home near Port Elizabeth. The main exhortation from Brother Nelson (an Australian) during school cricket nets was: "Boy, don't run away. Remember, you are British." But Thorne was endowed with natural sporting hand-eye coordination, great powers of observation and an instinctive appetite for the game, which enabled him to prosper in his age group to the extent that in 1948 he was selected for Western Province to the Nuffield schools week, a hotbed of youth talent, where he crossed swords with future greats Jackie McGlew, Trevor Goddard and Roy McLean. Despite failing to make the final select XI, his performances had raised him onto the fringes of the Border team and that unforgettable, brief duel with Hutton.

First-class cricket in South Africa was a very limited affair. There was simply not enough depth outside the major urban centres and – with the black communities excluded and the Afrikaner element largely uninterested – there were not the numbers or the money to sustain high-level competition. The Currie Cup provided inter-provincial competition in two divisions but this was suspended when England, Australia or New Zealand were touring, so first-class opportunities were in short supply and playing for a living was not possible. Thorne found employment with Barclays Bank and used his spare time and the meagre indulgences of his employers to gain experience in the game. With this employment came the compulsory signature on a pledge not to take any active role in politics.

Thorne's only top-level experiences in 1949–50 were two games against Australia. Neither brought conspicuous success, although the chance to watch Lindsay Hassett, Arthur Morris and Neil Harvey score centuries and share a South African XI dressing-room with Bruce Mitchell and Eric Rowan was unforgettable.

In 1950 he made the decision to head north. This was a career move based on dissatisfaction with his manager's attitude to cricket and a desire to try out the Government Miners' Training School near Johannesburg. Regular cricket for the South African Railway Club followed, as did advice – the first piece of coaching he had received – from Eric Rowan which enabled him to swing the ball both ways. But there was no first-class cricket for the two years of his stay as forcing a way into the Transvaal side was almost as difficult as gaining access to the national team.

Finally, in 1956, he returned to the first-class game in place of Osie Dawson, who was unable to find time for the "away tour" and Thorne immediately made an impact with 5 for 52 in a victory over Orange Free State in the B section of the Currie Cup, followed up with a pair of half-centuries against North-Eastern Transvaal. But then came two more seasons without competitive provincial cricket as MCC and Australian visits curtailed domestic competitions. The pleasure of facing an attack of Statham ("unbelievably quick"), Tyson, Laker ("the lift he got out of that plumb wicket was unbelievable"), Lock and Wardle ("I just couldn't pick his googly"), plus the batting of May and Cowdrey, and then scoring 95 unbeaten runs over two innings against Davidson, Kline

and Meckiff, was tempered by the difficulties of juggling sport, work and a young family. Forty-two wickets at 21.76 and 494 runs at 27.4 would normally have merited consideration for the national side, but the presence of Clive van Ryneveld and Trevor Goddard in a similar role – plus the fact that Natal and Transvaal were providing the bulk of the Test team – made the step up almost impossible. Perhaps there was also a slight lack of edge or ambition. Thorne was essentially a man who played for fun – to win, yes but also to enjoy the experience. Furthermore many leading cricketers such as John Waite, Tiger Lance and Jackie McGlew were either self-employed or had far more understanding employers, such as South African Breweries, who allowed them to concentrate more fully on their cricket.

Parallel to these seasons with Border was regular weekend sport at the Buffalo Cricket Club where Thorne shared a dressing-room with Donald Woods, a young reporter on the *Daily Dispatch* whose presence was to influence many lives and open many eyes. Brought up in the independent homeland of Transkei, Woods became a newspaper editor and then a pariah before fleeing the country in 1977 and having his story immortalised in the film *Cry Freedom*. This friendship proved a turning point. Previously Thorne had relied on his innate kindness and fairness in his relationships with people of all races but it had now become apparent that society had to change and impeccable personal behaviour would not be enough to bring this about. Mary Thorne worked as Woods' assistant secretary when he stood as an independent for parliament against

United Party candidate Clive van Ryneveld and the governing National Party, before Woods combined with Helen Suzman to form the Progressive Party (the first to press for true equality throughout the country irrespective of skin colour).

This increasing awareness of the iniquities of South African society did not, however, change the whites-only cricket in East London where segregation was allied to a lack of interest in cricket in the black community, unlike in Cape Town where a flourishing league produced players such as Tiffie Barnes and Basil D'Oliveira.

The seasons from 1959 to 1961 saw newly-promoted Border mixing with the powerful state sides. Thorne continued to make runs and take wickets but as the South African generation of McGlew, Waite and Tayfield began to leave the game there arrived a new generation, led by the Pollock brothers and Eddie Barlow. Peter Pollock was "sharp" and as for his brother Graeme, the only advice was simply not to bowl near his off stump. Barlow's confidence made him quite simply a force of nature.

Thorne was now playing the best cricket of his career, as a maiden first-class century and then 8 for 101 against John Reid's touring New Zealanders showed. But the time taken away from his family, an increase in responsibility at work and surrendering his annual leave every year to make the trip north for Border's away fixtures was proving an impossible juggling act. As Border's most reliable bowler he was also being given a huge workload – 179 overs in three games on the "away tour" of 1962 – meaning that supreme fitness was required and that took more time from his family. First-class retirement followed in 1965. As if to show that he was still a force to be reckoned with, his last provincial first-class game was a triumph reported by Donald Woods:

"But this was Robin Thorne's match. He took seven for 33 and three for 53 and scored 42 and 28. One of South Africa's most underrated batsmen, he is as soundly equipped with strokes and defence as anyone on the Border and his leg-side placing is precise. He first made his name as 'the boy who bowled Hutton' with the result that nobody seemed thereafter to take his batting seriously – except the bowlers who have toiled against him down the years. Yet although he is a good steady bowler and sound fielder it is as a batsman that Thorne touches the heights in cricket."

Just 44 first-class matches over 16 years is a sad indictment of the state of South African cricket at the time. This mish-mash approach goes part way to explaining the frustrating inconsistency of the national side before the golden generation briefly became world-beaters in the late 1960s. But Thorne achieved the aim of any self-respecting all-rounder, with 164 wickets costing just 20 apiece and a batting average 3.66 higher.

He continued to play club cricket for another four years but eventually even this became an impossible fit. He was then sent by Barclays to work in London just as the anti-apartheid movement was reaching full steam in its call for sporting exclusion. Thorne is categorical that this was the right move – economic sanctions were more likely to destabilise and depress the whole country but removing sporting links attacked the fabric of society without the vast economic effects that would inevitably trickle down to the lower levels, to those that were already suffering the worst of the system. For the same reason he was unenthusiastic, albeit understanding, of the pressure put on Ali Bacher over the rebel tours which failed to help black cricketers in any way.

Above all Thorne's was a career studded with friendships that grew into lifelong relationships: Ira Neuper, club colleague at Buffalo CC, who had survived five successful escapes as a POW and a death march from Munich to Auschwitz; the graceful and gentlemanly Osie Dawson, who played nine times for his country after winning the Military Cross; and Campbell Woods and Kevin Commins, who both offered generous and inspired help to a cricketer at the start of his career.

After retiring, Thorne decided that township coaching was the best way to give something back. He approached Ali Bacher who emphasised that the work was strictly voluntary, and he was promptly dispatched to Soweto. After four months he switched to Alexandra Township, an area described by Mike Atherton in 2010 as "five square miles of desperate degradation," and was again greeted by enthusiastic cricket novices. Within a month they had learned the fielding positions and enough of the game to play on turf and win at a whites-only school. Over the next four years

only one game was lost. It beggars belief that such progress could be made in such a short time and the effect this progress had on the self-belief of the young players can only be guessed at. One of the main aims was to discover talented black players for the Transvaal age-group sides and Walter Masimola fitted the bill and ended up playing for Gauteng and Transvaal Under-19s.

Not that it was all plain sailing. As a representative of the South Africa Cricket Union not everyone was keen on Thorne's presence and discretion was required when an armed opponent interrupted one session. But Thorne returned and within a year the two men were "friends".

These friendships continued as long as time would allow. John Ward of New Zealand, Jackie McGlew of South Africa, Alan Davidson of Australia, Tony Grieg of the world, and Donald Woods of campaigning journalism remained lifelong friends. With Mary by his side, Robin Thorne is happy to reflect on a life well spent.

Very sadly, shortly after receiving the news that this article had been accepted for publication, Robin passed away suddenly on 20 April. Earlier in the week he had been out on the golf course shooting his age. In his last email to me he said how honoured he was that people were interested in his cricket career and life – his primary concern had always been for his wife and two children. It is heartening to know that this small appreciation was so warmly received by its subject.

• • •

WHEN IT'S SO BAD,
IT'S GOOD

*PaajivsPunter on their masochistic relationship with
the dreadful Indian team of the 1990s*

The 1990s in Bangalore were quaint. Before "Bangalored" – losing one's job to outsourcing in India, specifically Bangalore – entered the global lexicon, it was a genteel town, content in itself. It had not grown to today's unmanageable extent: one could commute between two ends of the city within half an hour. Kids made their way to school every day armed with a half-ticket, heavy bag and lunchbox. Bangalore was also a lot cooler back then: hibernal reinforcements routinely appeared over school uniforms post-November. These scenes were quite common to most of urban India.

The proliferation of satellite television was not yet complete, even in the cities. Most of our classmates watched the same programming – designed by the state-run Doordarshan as a please-all approach, keeping a keen eye on a demographic-driven schedule. The post-school, early-evening slots were the preserve of school kids while general entertainment held sway later in the evenings and mythological serials brought the family together on weekends. Except when a politician died – resulting in state-wide mourning and the cancellation of regular programming – and kids across Bangalore were united in their grief for the loss of much-anticipated TV-watching time. Then, there was the cricket.

Cricket telecasts overriding routine programming was the lesser of two evils. Owning a television was still the preserve of rich and upper-middle-class folk, but communal consumption of Doordarshan's cricket broadcasts brought it to the masses. This is how many of us were introduced to the game. Discussing the latest match was routine, discovering unknown players through a stealthily arranged round of comparing Big Fun cricket cards was a guilty pursuit, rattling off Vaas's and Jadeja's light-year-long names was amusing,

and chattering about cricket in hushed tones – while pigtailed, red-ribboned, pinafore-clad girls sang patriotic songs – during school assembly was our first brush with rebellion.

One such song was *"Hum honge kaamyaab"*, which loosely translates as "we will be successful," and is set to the tune of "We Shall Overcome".

Hum honge kaamyaab, hum honge kaamyaab,

Hum honge kaamyaab ek din;

Ho ho man me hai vishwas, pura hai vishwas,

Hum honge kaamyaab ek din.

[We shall overcome, we shall overcome,

We shall overcome someday;

Deep in my heart, I do believe,

We shall overcome someday.]

The original – inspired by an early-20th century hymn – was a protest song during the Civil Rights Movement, popularised by folk singers such as Joan Baez. The phrase also found mention in speeches by Martin Luther King and Lyndon Johnson, and was later adopted by anti-communist protesters in the late 1980s.

The choice of words in the opening line is telling: *overcome*, signalling hope; *shall*, instead of the more definitive *will*. Pedantic, standard British English speakers will have taken note of the transgression with the first-person pronoun. Nevertheless, while "shall" represents strong intention, it is a more a gentle suggestion than the impolite assertion of "will". There was little room for nuance in the Hindi and Marathi versions though, which transform into the more explicit "we will be successful," and even less so in the Kannada and Bengali versions, which translate to "we will win." It was a brazen craving for success – not a hopeful wish to overcome odds. The desire for a destination rather than the journey.

No other song captured the mood of the Indian team's journey in the 1990s quite as effectively – more as a hopeful refrain from its fans than any promise shown by the team which stumbled from one overseas defeat to another. And yet, we supported them blindly. Patriotism perhaps? Past glory? The Indian team were no longer international cricket's whipping boys by the 1960s. Rapid strides were made in the '70s when they won away from home. The '80s saw a decline in Test-match fortunes, but one-day success more than made up for it with the 1983 World Cup win, the 1985 World Championship title and a semi-final appearance in the 1987 World Cup. Cricket had by this point poached a sizeable chunk of an audience who had grown up on heroic tales of India's eight Olympic hockey golds, but were now witness to apocalypse on AstroTurf. Hockey, a more time-friendly sport with a glorious winning tradition, had lost its audience to far less.

What chance did the Indian team of the 1990s have? The less said the better.

By all counts, it was Indian cricket's lowest ebb, and we are not taking into account whispers about match-fixing. India managed one overseas Test victory during the entire decade. *One*. That too against Sri Lanka, who had entered the Test arena just a decade earlier. With that win, India equalled Zimbabwe's record for the decade (Zimbabwe had won a Test against Pakistan in Peshawar). Did I mention, by the way, that we had lost away to Zimbabwe as well? In fact, in the '90s, India had the worst away record of the nine Test nations, both in win percentage and win-loss ratio. The only redeeming feature was an excellent home record where they won 17 and drew eight of their 30 Tests.

It was not just the losses that rankled, but the manner of abject surrender. Our batting meltdowns were the stuff of legend, with a lone fighting hand sometimes offering resistance on a burning deck: Sachin Tendulkar's insouciance at Johannesburg in 1992 (111 out of the team total of 227, next highest individual score 25); Kapil Dev's staged robbery at Port Elizabeth in the same series (129 out of 215, next highest 17); Tendulkar's spirited defiance at Birmingham in 1996 (122 out of 219, next highest 18); Tendulkar's and Mohammad Azharuddin's twin assault at Cape Town in 1997 (putting on a 222-run stand in 40 overs after being reduced to 58 for 5); that man Tendulkar again, tall amidst the ruins in Melbourne in 1999 (116 out of 238, next highest 31). These were the better times, when we had at least something to cheer about.

When it was bad, it was gut-wrenching.

Collective ineptitude came to the fore during a Test in Durban in 1996, when the team was subjected to tremendous pressure – perhaps enough pressure to form diamonds 800 miles west in Kimberley. The Indians obliged with totals of 100 and 66. The inability to chase 120 in Barbados in 1997 (only VVS Laxman managed double figures) was a body-blow to the nation's sporting psyche. On the Australian tour of 1999–2000, until Laxman made 167 in Sydney, Anil Kumble was India's third-highest run-maker (behind Tendulkar with 278 and Sourav Ganguly with 177).

Similarly, at home, when Tendulkar was dismissed 17 runs adrift of the target in 1999 with three wickets in hand, a sense of preordained gloom descended at the Chepauk, as the last rites of the match were conducted in front of our eyes by the Pakistani pallbearers. The Indian batting in Tests was abysmal – especially overseas – and the team were dismissed for a sub-250 score 23 times in 18 Tests in the '90s, of which – not surprisingly – they lost 15 and drew three. Granted, they had to cope with the Dukes and Kookaburra; some attributed our losses to a lack of balls altogether. We agreed.

The lack of match-winning bowlers proved to be the impediment to India's success in Tests. However, the limited-overs format did not hold such restrictions: India could now bank on outscoring the opposition. No team played as much ODI cricket as India during the decade. ODI series were a dime a dozen, named after fizzy drinks, cigarette brands, consumer electronics companies, and the odd motor company. Still, India's returns in the ODI scene during this fateful decade were middling at best. And the change of format didn't insulate us from the heartache of close losses.

The procession started with the two close losses in the 1992 World Cup against England and Australia. The second one was particularly agonising – five needed from four balls with two wickets in hand soon became three off the last ball, a run-out and a one-run defeat. India never really recovered from this start and limped right through the tournament to finish seventh; defeating Pakistan was the only consolation.

India lost several close matches (four by margins of under ten runs) and some big ones against Sri Lanka, including a collapse of seven for 21 in 1993; a collapse, a mini-recovery, and another collapse chasing 171 in 1998; and the most famous of them all during the 1996 World Cup semi-final after crowd trouble followed – wait for it – a collapse.

I know what you're thinking. What about the time Rajesh Chouhan smashed a six against Pakistan at Karachi in 1997? Or the Hrishikesh Kanitkar boundary in Dhaka during the Independence Cup final against Pakistan in Dhaka that won India the trophy? And the time Javagal Srinath and Kumble took us to victory in Bangalore against Australia in 1998? We beat Pakistan in the World Cups. Surely it wasn't all that bad?

I hear you and respond with: Basit Ali, Derek Crookes, Franklyn Rose, Stuart Law, Ali Brown, Matt Horne, Ricardo Powell, Peter Martin, Paul Adams, Henry Olonga – we made heroes out of all of them. A montage of *"Ghar Aaja Pardesi"* ("Return home, foreigner") from the *Dilwale Dulhaniya Le Jayenge* soundtrack greeted the performances of Shivnarine Chanderpaul, Dipak Patel and Ravindu Shah – players of Indian origin representing West Indies, New Zealand and Kenya respectively. We won only 17 of 45 games against Pakistan. But I digress.

May I interest you in a match – part of the same traumatic West Indies tour when we lost the Barbados Test in 1997 – where we lost 8 for 48 in eight overs, and the game? How about when we had the South Africans at 18 for 3 in 11 overs at Nairobi in 1999 and allowed them to amass 235? Generous Indian hospitality to the rescue? In return, we ensured we dutifully folded when we needed 46 from seven overs with five wickets in hand.

Should I go even lower? Alright, what about the time when a hobbling Salim Malik shepherded Pakistan to victory thanks to a 44-run stand in as many balls with Saqlain Mushtaq for the ninth wicket (Toronto, 1996)? Or the match where Manoj Prabhakar and Nayan Mongia inexplicably refused to chase 63 in 54 balls with five wickets in hand against West Indies in 1994? Then there's the 1999 World Cup vintage against Zimbabwe where we lost 3 for 3 with 7 needed off 11 and crashed out at the Super Six stage? Had we sunk any lower, we would have found enough oil to power us in the new millennium.

Unpleasant memories haunting you yet? Wait, there's more: Sidhu abandoning the team mid-tour in England; Ganguly tumbling over the ball and blinking at his fingers after a mis-field as if it were a difficult trigonometry problem; Ganguly again routinely running out a partner (you'd be hard-pressed to find any player for whom he'd sacrifice his wicket, Tendulkar included); PTSD-stricken Srinath underarming a throw from fine leg as the batsmen sauntered along for an additional run; and Venkatesh Prasad being dumped as nightwatchman, after his very first outing at that elevated position, in which he watched a ball travel all the way – to his stumps. (Gavaskar would've been proud.)

The fact that experts of the domestic game – including Karnataka players Dodda Ganesh and Sujith Somasunder – could not translate their performance to the global arena was especially frustrating for a Karnataka lad like me. My state had contributed eight players to the Indian team in the late '90s, and had won the Ranji trophy thrice over four seasons, but any expectations of international success were consistently dashed. Can you cast your mind back to the time when you eagerly awaited Somasunder's debut at the opening slot, only to see him score 16 from 63 balls over 2 ODIs?

It was in moments like these that a bond with Tendulkar was born, and cemented for life. Sure, he often crouched when he got bowled, and fiddled around his box too much. At times, he could retreat into his shell, as if batting under a hex. But most of us remember his defining image during the '90s: when it seemed as though he were walking on water.

Of course, there were other competent Indian batsmen before his time. Most would bide their time and distinguish themselves from the heap. Some could take on the bowling and briefly flicker before going into the night. But he was different. He illuminated the entire room, dispelling darkness and showing us light. Here was a boy with a curly mop, goofy grin and impish tricks up his sleeve, ready to take on the world in a way hitherto unknown to us. He was the wizard who waved the willowy wand.

Often, he would perform stunts that needed a parental advisory: he was a trapeze artist, human flame-thrower and a lion-tamer, all in one. We were the willing audience as our ringmaster capered down the track to dismiss the bowling, marvelling at the sheer audacity of his geometrical constructs as we grappled with humdrum geometry lessons.

Yet it was not just his cricketing feats that defined Tendulkar. Understanding why he stood on a pedestal in India's consciousness involves recognising the prevailing socio-political and economic milieu. Two prime ministers from the nation's first family had been assassinated in the space of seven years. No single political party enjoyed majority. The country's sovereignty was challenged at its north-western borders. The nation was bankrupt as every large-scale infrastructure project was funded by the World Bank. Millions were severely poor with no access to food, basic healthcare or primary education. Photographs of impoverished citizens and squalor routinely made the cover of Western magazines. Anybody with dreams and ambition made a beeline to go abroad. And why not? It beat standing in endless lines back home for essentials such as cooking gas and a telephone connection. Getting your hands on a two wheeler was akin to winning the lottery; stable employment in a government job was the only hope.

Cricket, at best, was labelled as a profligate pastime; at worst, an opiate conspiracy by the British to dullen and enslave the masses. The game was yet to see the kind of money that would make cricket a worthwhile profession to pursue in the eyes of Indian parents who pushed their kids towards medicine and engineering. Trenchant critics (like my father) would often invoke George Bernard Shaw's famous quote about cricket being a game played by 11 fools and watched by 11,000. Add to this the fact that the Indian team were terrible, stumbling as they did from one defeat to the next. Headlines like "Keen contest on the cards" metamorphosed to "Easy win for [India's opponent]" with worrying regularity.

• • •

Twenty-one players played fewer than five Tests for India in the decade. More than double that number played fewer than 20 one-day internationals. It reminds me of Tom Hanks's monologue as Chuck Noland in *Cast Away*:

> *"We both had done the math. Kelly added it all up and... knew she had to let me go. I added it up, and knew that I had... lost her. 'Cos I was never gonna get off that island. I was gonna die there, totally alone. I was gonna get sick, or get injured or something. The only choice I had, the only thing I could control was when, and how, and where it was going to happen. So... I made a rope and I went up to the summit, to hang myself. I had to test it, you know?....."*

Saying goodbye to cricket was quite difficult. We devised several coping mechanisms. Some of us turned capricious and moped, some took to gallows humour to enliven the moribund moments of the match, and others took to following other sports. Pete Sampras was on the horizon. So was Michael Schumacher. Manchester United seemed to keep on winning as we struggled to wrap our tongues around enunciating "Juventus" and "Sevilla".

We could now distribute our support, hope for someone to win at the end of the year and boost our morale, right? Could we give up on cricket altogether? Gulp. Lump in throat.

> *"....Of course. You know me. And the weight of the log, snapped the limb of the tree, so I-I – , I couldn't even kill myself the way I wanted to. I had power over nothing. And that's when this feeling came over me like a warm blanket. I knew, somehow, that I had to stay alive. Somehow. I had to keep breathing. Even though there was no reason to hope. And all my logic said that I would never see this place again..."*

Get busy living, or get busy dying.

It was Tendulkar's chutzpah that kept us going. Never mind that the rest of the team was terrible. As long as he was there, we had a chance. He seemed so happy to compete for the country – despite being amidst a sea of mediocrity – genuinely believing in our cause. And we, daft pricks, were contemplating abandoning the team. We sensed the electricity in the air when he took guard. He was our messiah who would bring forth our deliverance from the mess.

Of the 221 ODI innings Tendulkar played during that tumultuous decade, he crossed fifty 68 times. India won 46 of those matches – a whopping 75 per cent. There was daylight between him and second place (Azhar, with 27). The gulf in ability was starker in Tests: 25 fifty-plus scores away from home (13 each for Azhar and Dravid). Heck, he didn't even have to bat sometimes. He took two or more wickets in an ODI 16 times – India won 12 of those games. When he strode in to bowl that famous final over of the Hero Cup semi-final against South Africa in 1993, we knew something was up.

"...So that's what I did. I stayed alive. I kept breathing. And one day my logic was proven all wrong because the tide came in, and gave me a sail. And now, here I am. I'm back. In Memphis, talking to you. I have ice in my glass... And I've lost her all over again. I'm so sad that I don't have Kelly. But I'm so grateful that she was with me on that island. And I know what I have to do now. I gotta keep breathing. Because tomorrow the sun will rise. Who knows what the tide could bring."

And just like that, the tide would turn. After the match-fixing scandal, Ganguly led the team. No, it wasn't smooth sailing. There were several hiccups along the way. We would fall back on our old habits. We would make a hero out of Douglas Marillier. Our last three wickets couldn't last the extra half-hour that would have drowned out the result in the ten days of rain that followed against West Indies at Kingston in 2002 – we lost the series 2-1. Coasting at 159 for 5 after 34 overs, with 77 to get in 96 balls, we would somehow contrive to lose the TVS Cup final against Australia in 2003. We would drop Chris Cairns in the ICC Champions Trophy 2000 final, one of 14 ODI finals we lost under Ganguly. We would not choose to bat first after winning the toss in a World Cup final. C'est la vie.

But we will always have those two immortal matches: the 281 that would break both the Aussie juggernaut and Gavaskar's record 236 not out (India's cricketing equivalent of the four-minute mile) as well as the Natwest Series final against England in 2002. Both were accomplished with the minimal involvement of Tendulkar. He had served his time, and so had we. No doubt, we opened Pandora's Box every time we switched on the idiot box during the '90s, but what our parents never accounted for was Tendulkar being our Elpis – the spirit of hope in the Pandora myth. Quite simply, our hope fairy.

• • •

A collective chuckle emanated from the 1980s and '90s generation when MSK Prasad was recently appointed chairman of India's selection committee. Every member of the committee of five – before it was reduced to a three-member board by the Supreme Court – belonged to the same group of 21 and 43 who were part of India's musical-chairs decade. They were now in charge of the jukebox.

We smirk in a condescending manner when today's kids claim to be Indian cricket fans. They probably didn't switch off their televisions after Tendulkar was dismissed in the 2011 World Cup final. They treat victory with a sense of entitlement. They idolise Kohli, who offers certainty rather than hope. Must be fair-weather fans, no? Besides, where is the fun in that? What do they know of Indian cricket who do not the masochistic generation know?

• • •

A DAY IN THE LIFE

Jarrod Kimber hops the other side of the rope

The bench, the dug out, the change-room – entering the inner sanctum of cricket has been my dream since I realised that slow straight leg spin would not get me picked for Australia, or several levels below. The first time I tried to inch my way in, the ICC threw me off a team bus. At the time, I thought I might never get another chance, that I would stay forever a distrusted journalist, wondering what happened in the heat of battle.

Luckily for me, Cricket Hong Kong is one of the most progressive organisations in cricket, which is not saying much, but still. Their ex-CEO is a proper member of the cricket Twitterati, they have managed to start their own T20 league and get big players, and in only a few years they've changed the culture of cricket on the island. They had also once asked me to be their media manager, so I figured they liked me.

However, when they agreed that I could be with the team – for two List A games against the Netherlands – I had no real idea what to expect, how warmly I would be accepted, where I would sit, or how it would all work.

I was left just as confused when I arrived at the Tin Kwong recreation ground in Mong Kok, which is no different to any suburban cricket ground in the world except for the fact it's an international ground and has about 300 spanking-new apartments looking down over it. No one was at the gate when I arrived, partly because I had arrived well before the 9am start, and also because this was Associate cricket – things were different here.

After I'd walked around the ground once – and been none the wiser as to what was happening – Max Abbott, Cricket Hong Kong's marketing director, came up and gave me my lanyard. Then I met Charlie Burke, the godfather of the modern Hong Kong game and its outgoing director of cricket. He took me over to the Hong Kong tent to meet the team and support staff, and the head coach, Simon Cook.

The Dutch manager, Rob Kemming, saw me and came over. I had initially asked to sit on both benches, but after months of getting the odd polite reply but nothing approaching an answer, things got tense, a touch snippy. He told me how he had a personal bereavement and that was why he was a bit short with me. I didn't mention that I had contacted him four months ago. So I joked about how I would stay on this side of the tent, as far away from his team as possible (a feat I achieved so well that Peter Borren didn't even realise I was at the ground until he saw me at the hotel). The Dutch manager didn't take it as a joke.

I had no idea what I could and couldn't do other than not use my phone. So I switched it off and left it in my bag. Cook saw me standing around looking stupid, so he got me a chair. I now had the coach getting me a chair. The seating plan went analyst/coach, head coach, journalist.

Cook made me instantly comfortable and acted like it could not have been more normal for me to be there. But even so, for the first innings, I didn't move from the chair. Literally – I didn't go to the toilet, I didn't move around the tent at all, I stayed as far from the Dutch team as possible, and I tried to be seen rather than heard, which is not my normal state. I didn't even go and get my food until the Dutch team were seated eating theirs so that I didn't end up in the queue with any of them.

There are so many things I learned about coaching, analytics, role triangles, Associate cricket and leadership. Some things jumped out at me; I am programmed, like most journalists and cricket watchers, to look ahead. When Roelof van der Merwe began to hit out, I started calculating what he would do to the total if he took off, while the coaching team were looking into why they had the wrong player at point. They brought on a part-timer at the wrong time, and I wondered how much it would cost, while they wondered how they could make him a more effective bowler. They talked about how good it would be to give their captain an earpiece so they could give him constant feedback and advice; I wondered out loud to myself if that would change cricket for the worse.

There was no more chat here than you would get in a press box, it was just more frequent. There were no deadlines, there was no reason to shut up and, unlike in a press box, not every sentence spoken would get a retort. In this environment, endless streams of comments just disappeared. "Oh, Babar, don't do that," or "Why does he always scoop on a free hit?" just floated away, the rhetorical lament was king.

Sometimes it was like being in a regular cricket team. Someone got out early, and you didn't talk to him until he'd finished fuming, unless he talked to you first. The young kid kept being sent off on errands. The old scorer (or in this case analyst) made sarcastic comments when the players did or said something silly. The senior players held court; there were cliques, they laughed at one guy for being flashy. I could have been at a match watching some friends of mine play.

But then there was the use of modern sporting data, the run-rate queries, discussions of par scores, players who could look at their pitch maps, and a batsman who watched several replays of his dismissal. Not to mention seeing how a physio put together a split webbing, and then seeing it again two overs later when the tear reopened.

This game was an international and was being live streamed around the world, and there was a match referee behind me policing the game and what happened in my tent. There was gambling on this match; there were Anti-Corruption and Security Unit officers following it. And if I did the wrong thing, I could have caused an embarrassing incident for Cricket Hong Kong.

Plus I couldn't shake the idea that I was about to be thrown out. Someone from the ICC was going to contact someone at the ground and I'd be removed from the Players' and Match Officials' Area (PMOA) by security guards. The problem with making a film about corruption and mismanagement in cricket – and also making a career abusing or mocking the bad decisions that people make – is that you always think you're about to be kicked out. But no one came.

I made a decision never to go into the change-room; not through fear, but I figured the Hong Kong team accepting me so far was partly because I'd stayed at a healthy distance and that the change-room on match days was something you get invited into. But I did use the toilets, and on the way in I saw my ESPNcricinfo profile photo on the wall as one of the accepted people in the PMOA area. I would find out later that I was the media manager for Hong

Kong for this game, although as far as I knew, I was also the only media person in the ground.

There was a purity in watching the game with no distractions. I couldn't check my phone to see what someone was saying on Twitter. I couldn't start googling what a roles triangle was. No one could call me. I only missed the odd ball as I furiously tried to write notes on everything that happened around me. There were times when I forgot I wasn't part of the team, and I think if Hong Kong had more senior players (they had five teenagers in one game) I might have been put in my place a bit more. Instead, as one of the few adults in the tent, I was shown respect and even casually chatted to one player about his dismissal. I felt like part of the roles triangle, though I still didn't know what that triangle was.

My whole life I've loved talking cricket with cricket people. I was a slip fielder, a captain, and the guy in the dressing-room who continually wondered about every tactical move of the opposition. I knew early on that I was better at thinking and talking about cricket than I ever was at playing it.

I was at the MCG in November 1998 for Victoria v NSW. The MCG in November is not a busy place. The footy season has finished, Boxing Day is more than a month away, and there were fewer than 500 of us in the crowd. My seat was just by the dressing-rooms, and I was in the last row, with only the walkway behind me. And, with NSW doing well, I was getting annoyed. So I was talking and mumbling to myself.

Someone walked up behind me, and said, "What do you think of Corey

Richards?" I didn't even turn around, "It's not him I'm worrying about, it's this bowling, he doesn't move his feet to the pitch of the ball, so they keep bowling wide, he leaves most of them, and then occasionally smacks the over-pitched one through vacant covers. It's fucken bullshit." I turned to the man, who was in a suit and sporty sunglasses, and instantly realised I wasn't talking to just another frustrated cricket fan but to Australian chairman of selectors Trevor Hohns.

"Interesting. Think he can play, though?"

"Yes, but he's not the best on show in this match. Matthew Elliott was amazing against Tassie, he's a different class."

Hohns nodded, and we stayed there silently watching for a few minutes before he left. Elliott would bat twice in this match – against an attack that included Shane Lee, Stuart Clark and Stuart MacGill – and would make two incredible hundreds. For years my fantasy was that Hohns came up to me on day four of that match and we started talking about cricket. That he saw in me a mega-exciting cricket brain that could help him, and the team, and that I'd then done that for a living. It never occurred to me that the job I was fantasising about wouldn't even exist for another five years, and is still barely in use today.

So for me just being here with Hong Kong was pretty special. For Cook, though, I was just another part of being an Associate coach. Not only did he have to commentate during the game, but he also had to have a cricket journalist critique his every sentence and move (him playing with a plastic spoon made my cricinfo copy). He seemed to use me as a sounding board, another person to vent to when his players didn't listen.

By the second game, I might have felt like a member of the squad, but I still knew I wasn't doing anything that was helping the team. When Hong Kong collapsed in the second game, I realised how powerless the coach and support staff are. They tried to give out good, solid, simple information that could help their batsmen. And their batsmen went out there and played stupid shots repeatedly.

After Hong Kong's epic collapse, Cook chatted to the team and then sent them on their way. Afterwards, he came over to find me packing up. He started asking what I thought of the collapse, of what they could have done, and any sense I could make of it all. He could have just been happy to talk to someone who wasn't actually involved, but it was my dream come true. And I sat with an international coach and discussed what had just happened.

We finished chatting, he went into the change-room, and I went off to write my copy. I was still an outsider, but one with a taste of my dream.

• • •

OPENING WINDOWS

Stephen Connor on the joys – and pitfalls – of following cricket virtually

I'm suffering through a dull meeting in a nondescript municipal building in Livingston, in Scotland's central belt. The sun streams in through the window past the dangling vertical blinds. The topic at hand moves from the implementation of a new finance system to upcoming changes in European procurement legislation. My phone buzzes into life on the table in front of me. The preview indicates it's a message from a friend, but the screen is locked so I can't read it. I ignore the buzzing and look like I'm concentrating on the person speaking. Not long after, another message arrives, stinging the table once more with an angry vibration. The second interruption has now attracted the attention of other attendees – I apologise, switch the phone to silent and put it away in my bag.

It's shortly after 11am on the morning of 6 August 2015. While I'm at this meeting, several hundred miles south, the fourth Ashes Test is underway at Trent Bridge. I'm certain those messages mean something has happened. But what? An early wicket?

Or just a rain delay? But why a second message so soon after the first? Two wickets? An England collapse? Or news that Alastair Cook has launched a blistering assault on the Australian bowlers and is pinging sixes into the Radcliffe Road stand? These thoughts play on my mind for the remainder of the meeting. I'm reluctant to check my phone too obviously – the desire to keep abreast of the Test score is unlikely to be met with much sympathy in this part of Scotland.

Eventually the meeting ends. Walking through the car park, I scroll through the long string of silently delivered messages from the last couple of hours. "Rogers gone," "And another," "Jesus," "Broady!" And so, the story of Stuart Broad's astonishing demolition of Australia reveals itself through this series of punchy Whatsapp messages. As I climb into my car and drive back to Edinburgh, I think: "I can't wait to read all about this at lunchtime." This is how I follow cricket now.

• • •

Cricket writing is rooted in nostalgia and aesthetics. Most fans of such writing have enjoyed evocative descriptions from their formative years of following cricket: flowing cover drives, baking summers, Proustian packed lunches, reminiscences of watching heroes – Viv Richards swaggering to the crease (I've yet to read an account of him leaving a pavilion any other way) or cult figures mounting a rearguard in a Gillette Cup match. Every display of fast bowling or attacking strokeplay leaving an indelible mark on its observer.

I, too, have my own fond memories of watching cricket, both live and on TV. And yet, cricket for me is now almost entirely non-visual. I don't have Sky Sports and wouldn't have time to enjoy it even if I did. Family commitments and distance from a first-class county mean that I haven't been to a cricket match in nearly a decade. The background hum of *Test Match Special* is a joy, but it only goes on when certain circumstances allow – my three-year-old has surprisingly little time for Agnew and co.

But I still consider myself a keen cricket fan. I will be following England's Test matches this summer as avidly as before despite struggling to picture what most of the protagonists look like. My consumption is now mainly text-based, through websites and messaging services. This also means that – unlike the past, when I could dedicate myself to watching a game on holidays and weekends – it's at work that I'm now able to enjoy matches to the fullest extent.

Following a typical England Test involves three websites I've come to

rely on while the game is live. The first is Cricinfo, which provides live ball-by-ball text commentary with detailed descriptions of every delivery. This is factually correct and up-to-date information, a lynchpin to enjoying the game. Although a little dry, is it is the equivalent of watching a game live with the sound turned down. The facts are well presented but some of the context and flavour is missing.

The second site is the *Guardian*'s over-by-over coverage. More effusive and freewheeling than Cricinfo, the summary at the end of each over allows for more speculation and punditry than fits the former's ball-by-ball format. It lacks Cricinfo's speed and, to be honest, accuracy so it's important they complement one another. It is the text equivalent of listening to *Test Match Special* as it has the tendency to drift off topic and into more esoteric areas (generally around 1990s indie music). Like *TMS*, it has also developed a loyal community of followers with regular contributors and in-jokes.

The final part of my online enjoyment is Twitter. If the *Guardian* coverage is akin to *TMS*, then I suppose Twitter is more like a fan phone-in. It's not a direct comparison as that would be unimaginably awful. Thankfully you can restrict it to views that you respect. I've found that Twitter also has the pleasing side-benefit of highlighting a cricketing kinship with those you follow for other reasons. The result of the 2016 World Twenty20 final in Kolkata was relayed to me sooner than any news agency could manage – by comedian Al Murray ("Shit") and political commentator Alex Massie ("Oh England"). Seeing those words flash up on my screen was all it took to know it was over.

Incidentally, I've found the same superstitions persist even when I can't watch the game – the suspicion that you might be able to conjure a wicket by going to the toilet or making a cup of tea is just as strong. I've also found myself looking for non-existent tells in the relay of data that something exciting is happening. If, for example, Cricinfo takes a few seconds longer to update than usual, I brace myself for the fall of another wicket.

The fact that I rarely watch the game being played prompted me to wonder: what aspect of cricket am I actually enjoying? I'm not watching or even hearing any action, yet I'm clearly experiencing it live. But I'm just watching numbers change on a screen. How does that square with a game so steeped in notions of grace and beauty?

This is where the social aspect of social media is vital. Yes, it's important to know the score as it happens. But the knowledge that there are other people following the game, caring about what happens, is important too: the people that email messages to online ball-by-ball commentaries from work, the reaction of people on Twitter, text messages from friends, and this strange excitement and sense of belonging that can be felt even though we are all just staring at the same updates on our phones. Yes, it may be stupid but at least we are all doing it together. It lends my virtual pursuit legitimacy and purpose.

If you think about it, it isn't so unusual in the grand sweep of cricket's history

to follow the game like this. While cricket has been on television since the 1930s, coverage was patchy until the 1970s. The period of being a regular fixture on terrestrial TV, before being fenced off behind a paywall, was a glorious 30-year spell. But this period only coincides with a minor chunk of cricket's entire existence.

I feel like I have a vague sense of what it was like in the time before TV and radio coverage – relying on newspapers to print scorecards and provide comment. Only, rather than waiting two days for news from Australia, it is delivered in an instant. The need for instant gratification isn't necessarily conducive to great writing, but fans of cricket writing are not starved for choice or quality. Former players provide expert analysis and insight. The peerless Gideon Haigh provides intellectual and historical context. For a fan's perspective, the likes of Rob Smyth and Emma John provide gallows humour, honed through the mental scarring of following England in the 1990s. And it's now easier than ever to read the best cricket writing from other parts of the world. Want to know the about state of cricket in India or the Caribbean? In-depth analysis is a few clicks away. Who knows who in the future might be looked back on as a CB Fry or Neville Cardus?

• • •

The internet and social media allow the appreciation of fast and slow. It can indulge our frantic need to know now by keeping us constantly abreast no matter where we are – stood in the ruins of a cathedral (World Twenty20, 2016) or halfway up a mountain

(England v India, 2014). But it also allows time to reflect and explore niche interests. Since many of us are unable to watch the games any more, through either time or cost, match reports and analysis take on renewed importance. Good writers are required to tell us what we've just been following and to make sense of things.

Perhaps there has there been no better time to enjoy the game from a fan's point of view. And yet, I do have a worry. While I can't see the games any more, I do have a grounding in it – from watching TV and then being inspired to attend matches. I've seen the beauty of the game first-hand. When someone describes a shot as crisply driven or an edge being tickled, I have the stock footage to be able to reconstruct a mental picture. But could I ever say the same about my son? There are avenues for him to take up cricket (even in Scotland), but being in a club is a big commitment – one that I never took on. The future audience for

cricket can't just be those dedicated enough to get involved with cricket clubs. Where would he even find the inspiration to get involved? I have memories of watching games on TV with my father and brothers, glued to the screen, watching Michael Atherton face Allan Donald's ferocious bowling. Or summers spent listening to *TMS*, while the family drove to whatever holiday destination, wondering if Alex Tudor would complete his century (he didn't). What does my son have? A memory of his dad staring at his phone and occasionally punching the air. Not quite the same, is it?

Maybe there is some hope. With the ECB renewing their TV-rights deal later this year, there is speculation that at least some cricket might be available on free-to-air TV. Maybe one Sunday afternoon in the near future there will be a game on television that I can tempt my family into watching together – and have a chance to create some new memories.

· · ·

A MURAL IN TIME

Jonathan Liew dreams up Shane Warne's ultimate party

The film crew had been through almost every room of the house, and were just about to leave when the producer spotted the mural. At first, she thought nothing of it. Shane Warne's house in the Melbourne suburbs was like a shrine to bad art. The motivational posters featuring tropical sunsets and soaring eagles. The Matisse rip-offs that looked like a child's school macaroni project. The Barack Obama "Hope" poster, but with Merv Hughes in the main role. This, however, was on an entirely different scale.

The cameras started rolling. "I'll run you through a couple of the names," Warne said. "So there's Bruce Springsteen and myself just chilling in the corner, having a drink. Springsteen's got a cricket ball in his hand, he's just asking questions about cricket. The legend Mick Jagger, he's just sitting in the pool chilling. Then you've got Frank Sinatra and Muhammad Ali having a bit of a tune, just singing along. Then JFK's just mixing with Sharon Stone and Marilyn Monroe. Two of my closest friends, Chris Martin and Michael Clarke, just

having a bit of a chat. I tell you what, the artist has looked after Pup with those guns!"

When the programme eventually aired on Sky Sports in 2015 under the title "Shane Warne: Living the Dream", Warne was widely ridiculed for his vanity. Warne feigned indifference, but deep down he allowed himself a wry chuckle. Sure, he could be a touch outspoken at times, perhaps even unsubtle. But vanity was the last thing you could accuse him of. Besides, he knew the truth. The mural was not some fanciful imagining of an idealised poolside reverie. It had been painted from life.

• • •

Darkness washed over The Oval like a cruel sea. The champagne corks on the outfield would not be seen again until morning. The confetti danced alone. Moths flapped at the pavilion window, the only square of light left in the ground. Inside the Australian dressing-room, however, illumination offered no solace.

For much of the evening, they had laughed and drunk away the pain. The English came in to visit, but had not stayed long, eager to clamber into their waiting taxis and begin the festivities in earnest. And so the Australians commiserated alone, flipping open the bottles of Victoria Bitter that had been purchased for victory but would do just as well in defeat.

A taut and awful silence gripped the room. Simon Katich stared at the backs of his hands. Shaun Tait blew a one-note tune across the neck of his bottle. The silence was momentarily broken by a cricket ball rolling off the bench and hitting the floor with a thud.

"Well, fellas," Adam Gilchrist began suddenly. "At least we can tell our grandkids we played in the greatest Test series of all time."

Ricky Ponting harrumphed. "How can it be the greatest of all time?" he retorted. "We lost."

The click of a cigarette lighter interjected before Gilchrist could respond. From behind a tall stack of pizza boxes, the slumped and cetacean figure of Warne slowly winched itself upright. Warne inhaled slowly and exhaled with violence, an angry cloud of smoke pouring from his mouth.

"Yeah, we lost," he spat. "But we're still Australia. They won, but they'll wake up tomorrow morning and they'll still be England. Ian Bell will still be Ian Bell. Ashley Giles will still be Ashley Giles. The ginger bloke who came in and made seven, he'll still be the ginger bloke. Who's going to remember these guys in 20 years' time?"

Warne paused for effect. "Nobody, that's who," he said. He had developed a habit of answering his own rhetorical questions, a trait that grated on colleagues to an unfathomable degree, and which they would occasionally remark upon when he was out of earshot. But before they could dwell on their irritation, Warne continued.

"Yeah, they're having a bit of a party tonight," he said. "But if Warney throws a party, it's going to be the greatest party the world has ever seen."

Already, Warne's mind was racing quicker than his tongue could follow. Warne was often this way when a grand idea seized him: catalysed, almost to the point of breathlessness. "In fact," he continued, "that's what I'm going to do. Soon as we get back home. Biggest party in the southern hemisphere. Who's coming?"

Again, there was a certain sceptical silence. Every single person in that room had first-hand experience of one of Warne's "mega-parties". Invariably, they failed to live up to their advance billing. Often, spectacularly so. One time, the promised "A-list celebrities from the world of acting" had turned out to be Alf and Ailsa from "Home and Away". Then there was the time, a few years earlier, when most of the Australian team and their partners had turned up in anticipation of a "sumptuous moonlight dinner". When they arrived, they found that Warne's hot tub had been drained and filled with chips.

But it had been a long summer. Playing in the greatest series of all time takes a toll on the body, but it takes a toll on the mind as well. Nobody was in the mood to arrest Warne's flight of fancy. Many were already allowing their thoughts to wander homewards, to their own beds and home-cooked food and towels they had chosen themselves.

"You know those games where you have to pick your ideal party guests?" asked Warne, to nobody in particular. "Of course you do. Well, it'll be like that, except for real. Elvis Presley. James Dean. Frank Sinatra. Bruce Springsteen. Muhammad Ali. JFK. Marilyn Monroe. Princess Di."

It was at this point that John Buchanan, the coach, piped up: "Shane, you do realise half of these people are dead?"

Warne glowered at him. "Now that," he retorted, "is the sort of negative thinking that's been holding back Australian cricket for years. 'No nightwatchman.' 'No Hooters the night before a Test.' 'You can't invite this bloke to your party, mate, he's dead.' That's your problem: it's always 'can't' with you, John."

An unidentified yawn from the back of the dressing-room – it may have been Justin Langer, who had been up since 4am doing tai chi – seemed to spread like contagion. One by one, the Australians started stretching and rubbing their eyes and picking up their bags and drifting towards the door. "We'll have a barbecue," Warne announced as their descending footsteps cast echoes back up the stairs. "How's second week of October suit everyone?" But nobody was listening any more.

• • •

"Have you ever read *A Brief History of Time*?" Jason Gillespie asked. "Basically, it says that all time is a form of matter. It has a frequency and a position and a weight all of its own. If you could somehow create a gravitational field stronger than any field that currently exists in the universe, you could enter and exit the time curve at any point you choose. Are you going to have that side salad?"

Warne pushed the plate across the table, rapt in thought, or perhaps the lack of it. It was six months after the Ashes defeat and his party plans had yet to find any kind of definite shape. October had been a non-starter; most of the team had discovered immovable prior arrangements that prevented them from attending. So too November. December and January, at the height of the summer, were no good for anyone.

Meanwhile, a quick blast on Wikipedia had proven Buchanan right. Many of the prospective guests were now dead. But over a hastily arranged lunch in Fitzroy, Gillespie was enthusing about a potential solution.

"You know when you fizz one three feet outside leg stump?" Gillespie said. "And the ball kind of stops in the air? And it seems like time is standing still? That's not an effect. That's the gravitational field created by the revs on the ball. If you harness that, find a way to keep the ball spinning indefinitely, then essentially time is your servant. You can go wherever you want, in whatever direction you want, for as long as you want."

Warne looked unconvinced. It was not that the prospect of time travel was unappealing to him, or that the science underwhelmed him. It was more that he did not see the point. Why live 200 years in the future when you could live now, with the certainties of the present, when you knew where everything was in your fridge, and you had a pretty good idea what would be on TV that evening? Besides, people in the past would never have heard of him, and people in the future might already have forgotten him. He banished this last thought with a violent, involuntary shake of the head.

"What that means," Gillespie continued through a mouthful of rocket, "is that you can delve into history and grab anyone you want for this party of yours. JFK. Elvis. Leonardo da Vinci. Genghis Khan."

Warne nodded, a gesture that concealed a comprehension that was only partial. Over the months, the guest list had grown in his head. It now included Marlon Brando, Martin Luther King, Buddy Holly and Mother Teresa. But in his head it had remained, until Gillespie had called up out of the blue and asked to meet. Now he was talking about valvetrains and drive belts and hooking a spinning cricket ball up to his motorcycle engine.

"Remember the time I won a motorbike in that tour game in India?" Gillespie asked, spearing a radish with his fork. "It's still in the garage. So you attach the ball to the drive belt – that keeps it spinning – rig it up to a capacitor, beef up the hydraulics, spark it up, lift the throttle, and suddenly you're surfing the highways of time."

Warne pondered as he lit a cigarette. All sorts of thoughts were running through his head. What if Dizzy could actually pull this off? Even if he could go back in time and find JFK and Elvis Presley, how would he convince them to come to a party in Melbourne? And who was Genghis Khan? He could have sworn he had heard that name someplace. Indian? Off-spinner? 1950s? "Not famous enough," he thought to himself, and mentally scrawled his name off the guest list.

• • •

Once Gillespie got the bike running, things started to move pretty quickly. Warne sat pillion and operated the spinning motor: leggie to go back in time, slider to go forward. "It's so quiet," Gillespie remarked breathlessly as the years began to tick away, as the sharp edges and definite shapes of the garage around them began to blur and melt and warp and fade. The only sound was the ambient fizz of the Kookaburra ball behind them, wobbling furiously on its own axis, held in place only by its own eerie volition. "It's like a county game," Warne scoffed.

Some guests were easier to persuade than others. Mother Teresa refused on grounds of taste. Princess Diana offered her apologies, but she was due to be appearing in a haunting in Bristol later that afternoon and she had always prided herself on being a lady of her word. Buddy Holly had, for some reason, developed an aversion to long-distance travel. Monroe was sceptical, but agreed to come when she found out Kennedy would be there. Kennedy instantly agreed to come when he found out Monroe would be there. He told Jackie he was going to a Pacific trade summit.

But the big fish was Elvis Presley, who agreed to meet them at Graceland in 1972. Sprawled across his luxurious white-leather sofa, Presley refused point blank to accompany Warne and Gillespie to the future. The present was where his life was, and it contained all the food and prescription drugs and heartbreak he could ever want.

It took all Warne's powers of persuasion to lure Presley off his sofa and into the 21st century. "What are future generations going to say," he said in a vaguely scolding tone, "when they find out that the end of the world was coming, and you could have prevented it?" He paused for effect. "I think they'd find that pretty ordinary, if you ask me," he added.

• • •

And so, there it was. The weather was glorious, as glorious as it is in your dreams. Mick Jagger and Sharon Stone arrived first, having shared a cab together. "Incredible who you bump into in cosmetics," Stone remarked. Next came Jack Nicholson, bearing a giant slab of Victoria Bitter and with his 1998 Oscar for Best Actor in his pocket. He was followed in close order by Sean Connery. "Let me guess," Warne beamed. "Martini, shaken not stirred?"

"I'm driving," Connery grumbled. "Do us a Diet Coke for now."

Chris Martin was simply delighted to be there. Everyone he met was greeted with a fusillade of effusive compliments. "You're a fucking legend!" he shouted to Kennedy on meeting him. "I saw that Kevin Costner film about the Cuban Missile Crisis. I

mean, what an amazing experience that must have been. Just, you know, knowing how close we were to nuclear war. It would have been major. So fucking... fair play, man. Fair play. Do you like cricket?"

"Not as such, no," Kennedy replied.

Dimitri Mascarenhas looked, if anything, a little lost. He tried to strike up a conversation with Presley, but seeing as Mascarenhas had never listened to Presley's music and Presley had never watched a Hampshire CB40 game, their chat quickly fizzled out, and Mascarenhas spent most of the afternoon picking at a bowl of Doritos and wondering what on earth he was doing there.

Sinatra requested some music: "Connie Francis, if you have it." Warne said he would search his iTunes library but might have to resort to one of his playlists. Sinatra, polite to a fault, had no objections. And so it is that in the painting, the tune that Sinatra and Ali are belting out is "Somebody Told Me" by The Killers.

Warne circled the party in quiet contemplation, quietly marvelling at the tableau he had brought together. It all felt too surreal for words. Was that really Muhammad Ali reaching for the prawn skewers? Was that really Angelina Jolie lounged half-naked over a chair he had never seen before in his life? Was that really Anthony Hopkins in the character of Hannibal Lecter, flipping brains over on the barbecue?

In a funny way, he still had his doubts. Ever since he was young, he had always had a vivid imagination. It helped him as a bowler, too: not until late in his career did he realise that his ability to envisage what a batsman would do before he did it was not a skill all humans possessed, but a preternatural, almost supernatural, talent. There were times when he felt like an actor, in a film he had already seen many times before.

His reverie was broken by Martin, grabbing his shoulder and gushing about the ball that he had bowled to Andrew Strauss at Edgbaston. "It was fucking awesome," he said. "We were on tour all that summer and we've got the cricket on in the tour bus, and I'm sitting there thinking, 'fuck,' but it was an absolute genius ball. Seriously, what a genius. You, Freddie Flintoff and Curtly Ambrose are my absolute favourite cricketers of all time. And Botham, obviously. Martin Crowe. Lara. Shaun Pollock. Kumble. Sachin Tendulkar. What's he like to bowl at? I mean, Tendulkar, what a fucking genius..."

It had all gone more perfectly than Warne had dared to hope. Everybody was getting on famously. Sinatra and Michael Clarke exchanged telephone numbers and agreed to go for a drink the next time they were passing through the same spacetime. Bruce Springsteen learned how to bowl a googly and promised to teach the E Street Band when he got back home. Everybody was having so much fun, in fact, that nobody even noticed the two

large trucks pulling up outside the back gate; one bearing a giant water pump, the other carrying 150 industrial-sized bags of chips.

Later, after the last of the guests had left and the sun was finally receding, Warne went back inside the house. He saw his phone on the dining table, and instantly a cold dread settled over him. Even before unlocking the home screen, he knew what he would find. There were 19 missed calls and eight unread texts from Gillespie. He had been at the front door all day, pleading for someone to let him in.

• • •

"OK, that'll be a wrap," the producer announced, checking her phone for the time of her next shoot, a bunch of AFL players visiting a petting zoo in Collingwood. "That was great, thanks. We'll just take some cutaways of the exterior, and then we'll be out of your hair."

"No worries," Warne said, but the film crew were already opening the door by that point. Warne fancied he saw a couple of them smirking conspiratorially to each other. They left promptly and without a second glance, and so they did not see the cricket ball above the garage door, hovering a few inches below the ceiling, still furiously spinning.

• • •

Rock At The Oval 1972

MELODY MAKER POLL AWARDS CONCERT

SAT. 30. SEPT.
MIDDAY - 9 PM

EMERSON LAKE AND PALMER

Special Guest Stars

SHBONE ASH

GENESIS
FOCUS

Special ticket prices:
£1.00 in advance, £1.25 on day

...lequin Record Shops   The Oval
40 South Mo...

Ark Concert Presentations Present

Rock At The Oval 1972
PRODUCED BY RIKKI FARR

FRANK ZAPPA
HAWKWIND
SPECIAL GUESTS
JEFF BECK GROUP
LINDA LEWIS. BIGGLES. MAN.
SAM APPLE PIE
SAT. 16. SEPT. TICKETS £2·00
MIDDAY-9PM

Goodbye Summer

A Rock Concert in aid of the Victims of Bangla Desh
at the **Oval Cricket Ground**, Kennington, London, S.E.11
September 18th, 11 a.m. to 9.30 p.m.   (Gates open 9 a.m.)

THE WHO
ROD STEWART AND THE FACES

Mott the Hoople   Lindisfarne   Quintessence
+ Jeff Dexter   + Friends

Tickets now on sale. Price £1.25 at all branches of Harlequin Record Shops and all branches of
One Stop Records or by post from The Oval Cricket Ground, Kennington, London, S.E.11

HEAVY ROCK 'N' ROLLERS

Jon Hotten on the somewhat surprising glory years

In 1971, cricket's rock 'n' roll years were still half a decade away – Lillee and Thommo, Clive Lloyd's Windies war machine, Kerry Packer's funky clothes and floodlights all lay ahead. Rock 'n' roll's rock 'n' roll years, however, were in full swing. Led Zeppelin, Pink Floyd, The Who, Black Sabbath, ELP, Deep Purple, David Bowie, Yes, Neil Young and the rest were doing their thing. Jimi, Brian and Janis were fresh in the grave, already myths, with Jim Morrison, the Lizard King himself, bloated and dazed in Paris and just about to join them.

Yes, for rock 'n' roll 1971 was a rock 'n' roll year, perhaps *the* rock 'n' roll year. The music critic David Hepworth has published a bestselling book arguing exactly this point. If you were to plot the trajectories of cricket and rock 'n' roll on a graph, one was still flat-lining its way out of the '50s, barely touched by the cultural revolution raging around it, the other was burning towards its heady peak.

But then, why would you? Cricket and rock 'n' roll – and sport and music – existed in separate worlds, untouched by one another. It was hard to imagine Illy or Closey chatting about the Grateful Dead over their post-match pint, or Deadly and Knotty wearing flowers in their hair. The notion of a dashing cricketer was still caught up in the post-war heroism of Miller, the Brylcreem brilliance of Dexter and Compton. Yet it's not too fanciful to think that an impact was coming. A wild-haired quick bowler called Robert George Willis would take Dylan as an additional middle name, so deep and reverent was his love for the future Nobel laureate. The film *Fire in Babylon* revealed that Bob Marley gave Viv Richards his Rastafarian armband to wear as they approached the same issues from their different angles. Jeff Thomson, hair long, shirt slashed open, could have passed as a west-coast surf rocker every day of the week. His oppo DK Lillee, meanwhile, looked like any number of tearaway Aussie-bar band members – a small sample perhaps, but an inkling that those graph lines were likely to draw together with time. In the meantime, came a single extraordinary, if not entirely prescient, collision.

• • •

In 1971, Ray Foulk and his brothers Ron and Bill moved to London from the Isle of Wight. They had been on the island since Ray was 10, although they had boarded at Liverpool Blue Coat School, and in 1968, when Ray was 22, they'd put on the Great South Coast Pop Festivity, an all-night event that was headlined by Jefferson Airplane. The following year Ray booked Bob Dylan, and 150,000 people came. The year after that, 1970, the acts at the Isle of Wight festival included The Doors, The Who, Leonard Cohen, Miles Davis, Kris Kristofferson, Jethro Tull, Joni Mitchell, Joan Baez and Jimi Hendrix. Seven hundred thousand people rocked up and it became, along with Woodstock, one of the defining cultural events of the age. Mark Woodnutt, the MP for Isle of Wight, got a Private Members' Bill through the House of Commons which restricted the number of people attending any concert held on the island between midnight and 6am to no more than 5,000, and once the act was passed, the game was up. The Foulk brothers hit the mainland and began to look for venues in London large enough for their promotions.

Also in 1971, Surrey County Cricket Club were in financial purdah. The president, Maurice Allom, wrote to members to tell them that their "very survival" was at stake. The club secretary Geoffrey Howard knew that this was true. Although Howard was in many ways a traditional cricket administrator – he had managed England's Ashes tour in 1954–55, when they'd won in Australia for the first time since the Bodyline tour of 1932–33 – he was a forward-thinking man, once suggesting, during a committee meeting to which he'd worn a yellow shirt, that Surrey should have something similar made for their Sunday League games, and foreseeing a day when London

would have one cricket club and one ground. Howard and Surrey tried all they could think of to raise revenue: a Sunday market, a funfair, a bonfire-night event, and hosting Corinthian Casuals' home matches on the outfield. But nothing had worked, at least not well enough. As unlikely as a union between Geoffrey Howard and the Foulk brothers appeared, that was what happened.

"We were aware that they were pretty desperate for money," says Ray Foulk. "But we got on very well with Geoffrey Howard. His grandfather was Ebenezer Howard, who founded the Garden City movement, and I was into design and architecture, so it was all very agreeable."

Even so, the Foulk brothers were casting their net. They were in talks with Wembley Stadium, and as a first step were planning a show with Led Zeppelin at the Empire Pool (Zeppelin would play a famous two-night stand to almost 20,000 people, promoted by the Foulk brothers, in November 1971). "But the thing about cricket venues is they're more spacious than football. You can fit a lot more people in. We'd had trouble at the Isle of Wight, although it was exaggerated in the press, with people trying to tear the walls down, which were made of corrugated iron and scaffold. We'd had to build those. Ron liked the idea of walls built out of masonry.... I didn't know too much about cricket, but I remember being introduced to Geoffrey Boycott in the Oval car park. So I knew who Geoffrey was."

A guarantee of £3,000 secured the hire of the ground, although Howard needed to get permission from Prince Charles for The Oval to be used as a concert venue. Royal assent was forthcoming and the Foulks set about assembling a bill. The brothers had booked The Who for the Isle of Wight in 1969, shortly after Woodstock, where the band had also appeared. "They were feeling quite bullish about their position in the world," Foulk recalls, and when they heard about the fee the brothers were paying Bob Dylan ('£35,000 or whatever it was'), they had demanded an increase in their own money. Foulk found a way to bump up their fee, "and Pete Townshend was very gracious about it. He said to my brother: 'Well, we owe you one,' whatever that meant."

The Who appeared at Isle of Wight again in 1970 and the Foulks decided to approach them to headline the Oval show. "The management didn't want to know," Ray says. "We had Rod Stewart, who said he'd do it with The Faces but only if we got someone else big like The Who. So we went direct to Pete Townshend in the studio and persuaded him. He recognised that he owed us one and he agreed to do it."

To The Who and The Faces, Ron Foulk added Atomic Rooster, Eugene Wallace, Mott the Hoople, America, Lindisfarne, Quintessence, the Grease Band and Cochise. George Harrison had just organised the Concert for Bangladesh in New York, to raise funds and awareness of the refugee crisis during the Bangladesh liberation struggle, and the Foulk brothers decided to follow suit with the Oval show. In August 1971, posters began appearing around London advertising "Goodbye Summer – A Concert for Bangladesh". The date would be September 18, gates opening at 9am and the entertainment continuing until 9.30pm, all for the grand price of £1.25.

"And even then it got called expensive," Foulk says. "I mean we'd charged £3 for

the Isle of Wight, and you remember the bands we had there. People always complained, but if you allow for inflation, it's probably £25 or £30 today – which, for that line-up..."

After an international season that concluded at The Oval almost as dramatically as "Stairway to Heaven" with India's first Test win in England, and a county term that saw Surrey lift the Championship in defeat at Southampton, the ground made a new kind of history. Thirty-five thousand people came through the gates to find at the Vauxhall End not Geoff Arnold with new cherry in hand, but a giant stage erected by the Foulk brothers.

At 11am, the MC Jeff Dexter stepped on stage in cricket whites wielding a bat to introduce the first act of the day. Ten hours later, Keith Moon used the same bat to trash his drum kit, thus concluding both The Who's set, and the day's entertainment. "As you can see," Dexter told the crowd, "an encore is impossible. There are drums everywhere." Moon jettisoned the bat, which he'd used as a drumstick for The Who's opening number "Summertime Blues", into the crowd, much to Dexter's consternation – he'd borrowed it from somewhere in the pavilion.

"The Oval itself proved an ideal natural venue for staging a rock concert of this magnitude," ran the Melody Maker's review. "The unlikely partnership of the rock business and the establishment of the cricketing world paid off handsomely. At least £15,000 will be given to the Bangla Desh [sic] victims as a result. The choice of The Who and The Faces to finish off the night was a stroke of genius, not only because both rely on visual excitement to build up their act, but because there was undoubtedly a certain amount of rivalry between the two camps."

"It was a great occasion and the weather was OK," says Ray Foulk. "Then we did two the following year, and they weren't as hot..."

The summer of 1972 was a time of change, as the Foulk brothers were to discover. They had secured a date at Wembley Stadium along with two at The Oval, and found that "the bands were just not there". They had to fill Wembley with veteran American stars like Chuck Berry, Bo Diddley, Jerry Lee Lewis, Little Richard and Bill Haley and bill it as "the London Rock 'n' Roll Show".

"We thought of them as nostalgia acts," says Foulk. "The reality was they were only really 14 years on from their heyday. But people thought of them as passé."

At The Oval, they were co-promoting with a young Harvey Goldsmith. "We didn't get on well with Harvey's partner Michael Alfandari," says Foulk. "Philip Norman of the Sunday Times spent two weeks virtually living with us to write a piece and they used a picture of me having a stand-up row with Harvey and quoting my brother Bill as saying something like: 'The problem is it's the biggest show they've promoted and the smallest we've promoted.'"

For the first of the gigs, Foulk booked the brilliant but notoriously awkward Frank Zappa as headliner, with stoned-out space rockers Hawkwind as the main support act, along with (alleged) supergroup Beck, Bogart and Appice, plus Linda Lewis, Biggles, Man and Sam Apple Pie.

"Few people expected them to lose money," ran the report in the International Times, "but they certainly did – the factors being poor weather and expensive tickets – with the result that the green was never more than half full and the raised seating round the periphery hardly used."

"What was going on there was that whole kind of prog rock, intellectual side of hippy culture was becoming old-fashioned," says Foulk. "The new music was glam rock, coming in a big way. Anything to do with hippies was not a thing for young people any more. And Zappa had this kind of electric jazz orchestra..."

The second show, held two weeks later on September 30, was the Melody Maker's Poll Awards concert. Disconcertingly for Ray Foulk, the poll had been won by ELP, who were most certainly a prog-rock band. Their support came from the guitar-heavy Wishbone Ash and Focus, and another emerging progressive rock act, Genesis.

"The only place where we'd appeared at any sort of arena was Italy," says Steve Hackett, who played guitar with Genesis from 1970 until 1977. "It was only there that we had that sort of pull. For some reason we were big in Italy almost from day one. Nobody really knows why. We certainly weren't in England."

In November of 1971, Genesis had released Nursery Cryme, their now-classic third album and the first to feature Hackett's revelatory, dextrous playing. Foxtrot, the record that would make their name, followed weeks after the Oval show. They were young men, on the cusp of something – what it was, they weren't quite sure.

"It was a very sunny day," Hackett says. "Focus were on just before us and they were very good. I had a feeling of trepidation. Jan Akkerman played very well – he was their guitarist at the time. We played our set and went down moderately well, and I remember seeing ELP, the young ELP. Keith [Emerson] was at his showman best, and Greg Lake sounded amazing. The last time I'd seen him was with King Crimson in '69... Keith had one of those synthesisers that looked like an old telephone exchange, with wires in the back, and this plank thing that made noises that he took down the front and waved around like a penis."

Hackett had joined Genesis after placing a classified ad in *Melody Maker* seeking musicians that wanted to "strive beyond existing stagnant forms". He was the studious sort: "My cricket skills were negligible, although my dad was both a very good cricketer and footballer. But I wore glasses, and in those days glasses were made with glass, and so I felt very exposed playing cricket. I was at school with Malcolm Macdonald and not only was he very good as a footballer, he was also captain of the cricket team, and he was a fast bowler. God, I wanted to be a fast bowler."

Before 16,000 people at The Oval, Hackett at least got to come on from the Vauxhall End.

The show recouped some of the losses, both financial and of reputation, from the Zappa gig two weeks before, which had overrun the 10pm curfew and seen bonfires lit on the outfield. The closest ELP came to that was the Tarkus stage prop, a giant aluminium and felt representation of William Neal's cover painting for the album of the same name, an oversized armadillo with machine guns for arms (well, it was 1972...).

"ELP did better, certainly," says Ray Foulk. "But it still wasn't very strong financially. And of course ELP and Genesis went on to great success around the world. We got distracted about the same time by Milton Keynes, where we became advisors on their leisure programme. It was ridiculous because we didn't have a clue but they thought we were big names. But what they were doing was exciting – this whole plan-produced city."

Ray Foulk spent the next three years working with Milton Keynes, helping to develop the Bowl, before starting a successful career as an architect. Geoffrey Howard steered Surrey through its financial crisis, serving as secretary until 1975, and as club president in 1989. After a fatality at a show in Crystal Palace, Lambeth Council introduced a regulation that the number of tickets sold for any show within the borough could not exceed the number of seats at the venue, making any further concerts at The Oval impossible.

To date, Emerson Lake and Palmer remain the final band to have gigged on the outfield. But in the summer that saw the first Glastonbury Festival and BS Chandrasekhar's finest hours, The Oval was an unlikely home for great deeds from very different heroes.

Ray Foulk's memoir, Stealing Dylan From Woodstock, *is published by Medina. Steve Hackett's latest album is* The Night Siren (Inside Out). *He tours the UK and Europe this year. For details visit www. hackettsongs.com. Thanks to www. ukrockfestivals.com.*

• • •

CONTRIBUTORS

Tanya Aldred is a freelance writer and co-editor of *The Nightwatchman*. She can't work out whether she's becoming increasingly anti-social or if cricket is a bit in your face these days. Her children tell her she's just getting old.

Luke Alfred is a long-time journalist and author. His most recent book is *Early One Sunday Morning I Decided to Step Out and Find South Africa*. The story of 12 hikes and rambles across South Africa he undertook in a calendar year, the book was a thorough departure from the game he loves. It contained no references to cricket whatsoever.

Lawrence Booth edits *Wisden* and writes about cricket for the *Daily Mail*. He hopes one day to score a hundred in his only first-class innings.

Tim Cooke is a teacher and freelance journalist. He writes about books, films, education and travel for various publications, including the *Guardian*, *Little White Lies*, *The Quietus*, *Ernest Journal* and the *Hackney Citizen*. His creative work has appeared in the *Lampeter Review*, *Stepz* and *Litro Magazine*.

Stephen Connor is procurement professional based in Edinburgh. He's also a keen cricket fan, occasional whisky blogger and very occasional cricketer. Follow him @whiskywriter.

Liam Cromar is a lover of slow cricket who's partial to the odd portion of speed cricket. His current mania is a limited-overs/declaration mash-up format, which he inflicts on Haymakers CC at every opportunity. His work has featured on ESPNcricinfo and in *Wisden* and *The Cricketer*. He aspires to being a real cricket writer someday. Find him muttering to himself on @LiamCromar, shaking his head in the Edrich, or missing catches at mid-off on a Herefordshire cricket field.

Paul Edwards is a freelance cricket writer who works for *The Times*, ESPNcricinfo, *The Cricketer*, *All Out Cricket*, *Wisden Cricketers' Almanack* and many other publications. At an age when many of his contemporaries had a photograph of a female tennis player scratching her left buttock on their walls, Paul preferred to look at a picture of FS Jackson playing an off-drive.

Patrick Ferriday was indoctrinated by his art-historian father Peter on tales of Phil Mead and Denis Compton. His first book, *Before the Lights Went Out: the 1912 Triangular Tournament*, was shortlisted for the MCC/Cricket Society award. He has also edited, published and contributed to *Masterly Batting* and *Supreme Bowling*, which tell the tale of the 100 greatest Test centuries and 100 greatest bowling performances. He lives in Brighton, laments the current Sussex team

and his real job is as horse-racing commentator and abysmal punter.

Peter Hanlon wrote and edited sport for *The Age* in Melbourne for more than 20 years and enjoyed two stints working on Fleet Street. During the second, an exchange posting at the *Guardian* which coincided with the 1998–99 Ashes, a modest and gentle sub-editor thanked him for not crowing about England's defeat. It's probably his proudest moment in journalism.

Tristan Holme spent his youth sneaking into Harare Sports Club by vaulting the fence next to the swimming pool, and remains in touch with the game in Zimbabwe. But with Zimbabwe cricket in a coma, he is biding his time in Cape Town where he currently serves as South Africa correspondent for Cricbuzz. @tristanholme

Jon Hotten worked for *Kerrang!* magazine from 1987 to 1994 (the glory years of heavy metal, as anyone will tell you). He's the author of four books, including *The Meaning of Cricket* and *My Life and the Beautiful Music*. @theoldbatsman

Jarrod Kimber is the global writer for ESPNcricinfo, co-directed *Death of a Gentleman*, wrote *Test Cricket: the Unauthorised Biography* and has done other stuff too.

Noah Levick is a recent graduate of Bates College in Lewiston, Maine, and an aspiring sports writer. The former editor-in-chief of *The Bates Student*, he has also written for the *Portland Press Herald*, *Whistle*, and CSNPhilly. com. He is a proud native of Philadelphia, Pennsylvania.

Jonathan Liew is a sportswriter for the *Telegraph* whose work has also appeared in *The Cricketer*, *Wisden* and the *Cricket Monthly*. He lives in south London, a short walk from The Oval (a detail that it would have been far more appropriate to include in the Oval issue, had he not unfortunately missed the deadline). He tweets at @jonathanliew.

SJ Litherland's seventh collection of poetry *Composition in White* is due from Smokestack Books in October. Her new book is about England, cricket and a Warwickshire childhood with left-wing sentiments. She's an irate member of Durham County Cricket Club.

Benj Moorehead is a freelance writer and editor of the *Cricketers' Who's Who*. He worked for *The Cricketer* magazine from 2008 to 2014, much of that time spent travelling far and wide to watch village cricket in a red Nissan Micra with his German wife. He currently lives in Italy (mostly).

PaajivsPunter is an anonymous collaborative cricket blog. The name originates from the subject of an email thread between Indian cricket followers in December 2010 when Sachin Tendulkar found a second wind and leapt ahead of the pack (including Ponting) chasing him. PaajivsPunter have contributed to several publications, including *Mint*, *the Hindu*, scroll.in, and firstpost.com.

James Runcie is a writer, director and literary curator. He is the author of *The Grantchester Mysteries*, a Fellow of the Royal Society of Literature, Visiting Professor at Bath Spa University, and the Commissioning Editor for Arts at BBC Radio 4. He was a founder member of *The Late Show*. His father, Lord Robert Runcie, former Archbishop of Canterbury, gave the address at the *Wisden* dinner in 1997 and James followed suit this year. @james_runcie

Bharat Sundaresan is a cricket writer with the *Indian Express* who spends as much time making sure his mane looks its best as he does writing about everything cricket.

Jaideep Varma is the founder of Impact Index, a statistical system in cricket. Impact Index recently published their first book, with former cricketer and current cricket writer and commentator Aakash Chopra, called *Numbers Do Lie: 61 Hidden Cricket Stories* (HarperCollins). The essence of Varma's piece in this issue is elaborated upon in detail in the book.

Yvette Walker is an Australian writer hiding out in rural New Zealand. Her debut novel *Letters to the End of Love* won a West Australian Premier's Book Award. She is working on the difficult second novel. Her Proustian moment will always be a perfect off-drive for four during a long-ago university cricket match. @ywalkerwriter

. . .

THE Nightwatchman

THE WISDEN CRICKET QUARTERLY

ISSUE **19**

The nineteenth issue of *The Nightwatchman* will be out in early September and will focus on *Test Match Special*, celebrating 60 years in 2017.

If you have an article you would like to see appear in this special issue of *The Nightwatchman*, let us know by contacting us at editor@thenightwatchman.net

Smile
Group Travel

Ashes Series 2017-18
(Nov-Jan)

New Zealand 2018
(Feb-Apr)

Sri Lanka 2018
(Oct-Nov)

2017-18 Hosted Supporters Tours

Our tours are always hosted by ex-professional players such as Devon Malcolm and Don Topley. Together with our support staff, they will ensure that supporters have the most interesting and exciting tour experience.

Our supporters will also be able to meet and socialise with many other past & present players at our spectacular tour social events.

"Would I use Smile again? I wouldn't use anyone else!"
George Dobell, Senior Correspondent, ESPN Cricinfo

Playing Tours

Smile Group Travel have over 10 years' experience in the group travel industry. We also offer the most exciting playing tours to every destination for cricketers of all ages.

"Another wonderful trip with Smile. All of my fussy demands were met and the whole tour was an absolute breeze! Smile are so easy to deal with and I couldn't recommend anyone more highly to tour with!"
Phil Lewis, Director of Cricket, Kings College Taunton

info@smilegrouptravel.com   01708 893 250   www.smilegrouptravel.com